Traditional
BRITISH
COOKING

Traditional BRITISH COOKING

Audrey Ellis

Photographed by Robert Golden

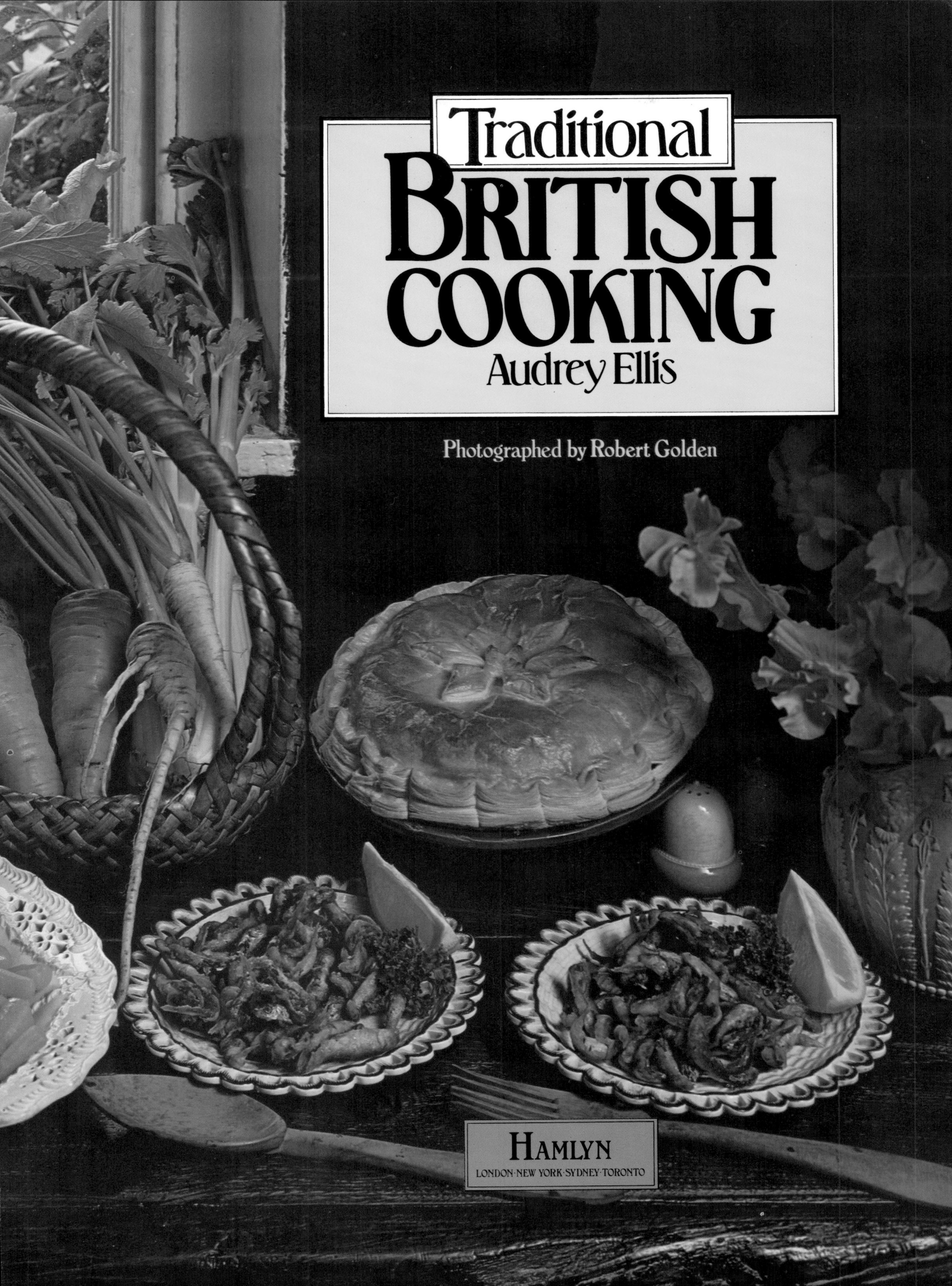

HAMLYN
LONDON · NEW YORK · SYDNEY · TORONTO

Acknowledgements

The author would like to thank the following for their kindness in supplying traditional family recipes: Mrs Alma Addison of Thornaby; Mrs Mabel Dart of Grimscott; Miss Evelyn Gray of Linby; Mrs Alwyn Little of Acklam; Mrs Joan Montgomery of Edinburgh; Miss Jean Mulholland of Middlesbrough; Mrs Edna Redhead of Plymouth; Mrs Edith Wynne-Ellis of Llandudno; also Mrs Minwell Tibbott, Assistant Keeper of the Welsh Folk Museum, and Mrs Joy Davies of London who conducted much patient research for this book.

The Publishers would like to thank the following for the kind loan of accessories for photography: Craftsmen Potters Association, Marshall Street, London W1; Leon Jaeggi & Sons Ltd, 232 Tottenham Court Road, London W1; Reject China Shop, 33 Beauchamp Place, London SW3; Reject Shop, 209 Tottenham Court Road, London W1; Welsh Craft Centre, 242 Brompton Road, London SW3.

Also Mr and Mrs Ince, for the kind use of their home and garden; and Egham Cricket Club.

The Publishers would also like to thank the following for the use of their colour photographs: John Bethell, page 46; Bruce Coleman – Peter Loughran, page 58; Bruce Coleman – Colin Molyneux, page 38; Bruce Coleman – Trevor Wood, page 90; Mike St. Maur Sheil, page 74; Kenneth Scowen, page 138; Tony Stone Associates, pages 14 and 122; Pamela Toler, page 110.

Black and white line illustrations by courtesy of Dover Publications, Inc., New York.

Cover photograph by James Jackson

First published in 1979 under the title of
The Great Country Cookbook

This edition published in 1983 by
The Hamlyn Publishing Group Limited
London · New York · Sydney · Toronto
Astronaut House, Feltham, Middlesex, England

Reprinted 1984

ISBN 0 600 32439 7

Phototypeset in Garamond 10/11pt by Tradespools Limited,
Frome, Somerset
Printed in Hong Kong

Contents

BRITISH ISLES
NORTH SEA
GERMAN OCEAN
OR
ATLANTIC OCEAN
SHETLAND ISLANDS
ORKNEY ISLANDS
IRISH SEA
ST. GEORGE'S CHANNEL
BRISTOL CHANNEL
THE NORTH CHANNEL
SOUTH WALES
BRITISH

Introduction

The map of Britain stretches out before the eye, county by county, like a vast patchwork quilt. I have always seen it in the soft colours of nature, ranging through innumerable green shades of grassland and forest, the golds of ripe grain, to the misty greys and purples of granite and heather.

Each region according to its geography has a character and history of cooking all its own. Dishes which are local specialities have evolved partly because of climate and agriculture, and partly from historical changes like invasion from abroad and the growth of industry.

Some remote areas have remained virtually untouched by time. Those ancient Britons who surrendered to Roman invaders, were first astonished by their sophisticated cooking techniques and subtle ingredients, then gradually came to adopt them. But the Roman influence reached no further north than Hadrian's Wall. Wily Scots set fire to the heather to create a diversion while they stole the garrisoned legion's horses. They probably cooked oatcakes before the foray on a hot hearthstone, or on an iron girdle over the open fire. Both the food and the method of cooking have hardly altered. It is interesting that where the Roman penetration was weakest (in the extreme North of England, in Wales and Ireland) this basic form of cooking is still so popular today. The flat iron plate is called a girdle by Scots, a bakestone or planc by the Welsh, and a griddle by cooks in Northern England and Ireland. But it is virtually the same simple utensil originally used over an open fire.

Closer to London, the influence of successive invaders, especially the Normans, has always been most strongly felt, and foreign ideas about food easily assimilated. The dense population of the South and South East of England invited innovations. When large towns with thriving markets grew up close together in populous areas, tradesman-cooks, such as the baker and pie-maker, answered the demand for more elaborate fare than any local housewife could offer her family. Vendors of expensive imported foods, such as spices from Egypt and dried figs from Smyrna, travelled from one market to another, always sure to find a throng of purchasers for their wares.

As different methods of cooking and a wider choice of ingredients became familiar, so did home cooking improve and become less monotonous; always combining what was strange with the well known and loved local produce. Enterprising importers and merchants rarely found their way to the deserted glens and lochs of Northern Scotland, where in any case big towns and heavy purses were rare.

Industry has also been responsible for many changes in cooking. When it forced large numbers of people to live huddled in close proximity to the factory, mine or mill, they came to use mass-produced food rather than cooking everything for themselves. A housewife began to rely on the baker's loaf more than on her own bag of flour. And this trend has continued, although in many cases regional dishes stubbornly survive. Selkirk Bannock and Sussex Pond Pudding are two such glorious survivors.

That is what makes the cooking of our islands so interesting and varied; the imprint of historical events on regional riches producing many distinct and delightful results in the kitchen. This is a personal selection of recipes which I believe conveys the flavour of each region's cooking.

Audrey Ellis

USEFUL FACTS AND FIGURES

Notes on metrication

In this book quantities are given in metric and Imperial measures. Exact conversion from Imperial to metric measures does not usually give very convenient working quantities and so the metric measures have been rounded off into units of 25 grams. The table below shows the recommended equivalents.

Ounces	Approx g to nearest whole figure	Recommended conversion to nearest unit of 25
1	28	25
2	57	50
3	85	75
4	113	100
5	142	150
6	170	175
7	198	200
8	227	225
9	255	250
10	283	275
11	312	300
12	340	350
13	368	375
14	396	400
15	425	425
16 (1 lb)	454	450
17	482	475
18	510	500
19	539	550
20 (1¼ lb)	567	575

Note: When converting quantities over 20 oz first add the appropriate figures in the centre column, then adjust to the nearest unit of 25. As a general guide, 1 kg (1000 g) equals 2.2 lb or about 2 lb 3 oz. This method of conversion gives good results in nearly all cases, although in certain pastry and cake recipes a more accurate conversion is sometimes necessary to produce a balanced recipe.

Spoon measures All spoon measures given in this book are level unless otherwise stated.

Liquid measures The millilitre has been used in this book and the following table gives a few examples.

Imperial	Approx ml to nearest whole figure	Recommended ml
¼ pint	142	150 ml
½ pint	283	300 ml
¾ pint	425	450 ml
1 pint	567	600 ml
1½ pints	851	900 ml
1¾ pints	992	1000 ml (1 litre)

Herbs The herbs used in the recipes are fresh unless specified otherwise.
Flour Unless specified, either plain or self-raising flour can be used in the recipes.
Fats Many of the authentic old recipes use lard. For modern taste, butter or margarine can be satisfactorily substituted for part of or the whole quantity.
Yeast If using dried yeast substitute half the stated quantity for fresh and follow the instructions on the packet.

Oven temperatures

The table below gives recommended equivalents.

	°C	°F	Gas Mark
Very cool	110	225	¼
	120	250	½
Cool	140	275	1
	150	300	2
Moderate	160	325	3
	180	350	4
Moderately hot	190	375	5
	200	400	6
Hot	220	425	7
	230	450	8
Very hot	240	475	9

Notes for American and Australian users

In America the 8-oz measuring cup is used. In Australia metric measures are now used in conjunction with the standard 250-ml measuring cup. The Imperial pint, used in Britain and Australia, is 20 fl oz, while the American pint is 16 fl oz. It is important to remember that the Australian tablespoon differs from both the British and American tablespoons; the table below gives a comparison. The British standard tablespoon, which has been used throughout this book, holds 17.7 ml, the American 14.2 ml, and the Australian 20 ml. A teaspoon holds approximately 5 ml in all three countries.

British	American	Australian
1 teaspoon	1 teaspoon	1 teaspoon
1 tbl/spoon	1 tbl/spoon	1 tbl/spoon
2 tbl/spoons	3 tbl/spoons	2 tbl/spoons
3½ tbl/spoons	4 tbl/spoons	3 tbl/spoons
4 tbl/spoons	5 tbl/spoons	3½ tbl/spoons

An Imperial/American guide to solid and liquid measures

Solid measures

Imperial	American
1 lb butter or margarine	2 cups
1 lb flour	4 cups
1 lb granulated or castor sugar	2 cups
1 lb icing sugar	3 cups
8 oz rice	1 cup

Liquid measures

Imperial	American
¼ pint liquid	⅔ cup liquid
½ pint	1¼ cups
¾ pint	2 cups
1 pint	2½ cups
1½ pints	3¾ cups
2 pints	5 cups (2½ pints)

Note: WHEN MAKING ANY OF THE RECIPES IN THIS BOOK, ONLY FOLLOW ONE SET OF MEASURES AS THEY ARE NOT INTERCHANGEABLE.

American terms

The list below gives some American equivalents or substitutes for terms and ingredients used in this book.

Equipment and terms

British/American
baking tray/baking sheet
base/bottom
cocktail stick/toothpick
deep cake tin/spring form pan
double saucepan/double boiler
dough or mixture/batter
flan tin/pie pan
frying pan/skillet
greaseproof paper/wax paper
grill/broil
gut fish/clean fish
hard-boil eggs/hard-cook eggs
liquidiser/blender
loaf tin/loaf pan
minced/ground
muslin/cheesecloth
pastry or biscuit cutter/cookie cutter
patty or bun tins/muffin pans or cups
piping bag/pastry bag
polythene/plastic
prove dough/rise dough
pudding basin/ovenproof bowl or pudding mold
roasting tin/roasting pan
sandwich tin/layer cake pan
stoned/pitted
sugar thermometer/candy thermometer
Swiss roll tin/jelly roll pan
top and tail fruit/stem fruit
whisk eggs/beat eggs

Ingredients

British/American
apple, cooking/apple, baking
bacon rashers/bacon slices
beef suet, shredded/beef suet, chopped
bicarbonate of soda/baking soda
biscuits/crackers or cookies
biscuit mixture/cookie dough
black cherries/bing cherries
black pudding/blood sausage
black treacle/molasses
boiling fowl/stewing chicken
cake mixture/cake batter
celery stick/celery stalk
chocolate, plain/chocolate, semi-sweet
cocoa powder/unsweetened cocoa
coconut, desiccated/coconut, shredded
cornflour/cornstarch
cream, single/cream, light
cream, double/cream, heavy
essence/extract
flour, plain/flour, all-purpose
flour, self-raising/flour, all-purpose sifted with baking powder
glacé cherries/candied cherries
ham/cooked ham
icing/frosting
lard/shortening
marzipan/almond paste
shortcrust pastry/basic pie dough
raisins, seedless/raisins, seeded
scones/biscuits
semolina/semolina flour
shrimps or prawns, peeled/shrimp, shelled
soured cream/sour cream
spring onion/scallion
stock cube/bouillon cube
sugar, icing/sugar, confectioners'
sultanas/seedless white raisins
swede/rutabaga
tomato purée/tomato paste
vanilla pod/vanilla bean
yeast, fresh (25 g/1 oz)/yeast, compressed (1 cake)

SCOTLAND

Scottish cooking is based on the products of a bleaker, wilder terrain than any other in the British Isles. Early-ripening crops of oats and barley flourish in the Highlands where wheat would wither on the stalk before it could be harvested. Flour is still looked on as a precious commodity there, and the staple foods are fish and oatmeal.

Scotland is a country of contrasts. The simple, almost primitive cooking of the sparsely populated North reflects the harsh difference in climate between this region of solitary crofts perched on precipitous and almost barren hillsides, and the milder, more productive and industrial South.

A crofter's wife often lives in sight of the sea, a river or loch. She gets her share of freshly caught silver darlings (the herrings which swarm round Scotland's ragged coastline), trout from the burn, or salmon. At times, there's plenty of game for the pot; venison, hare and rabbit, grouse, pheasant and capercailzie. Milk and meat have to come from the few beasts a small farm sustains, other than the main source of income, a flock of hardy, sure-footed sheep. But in winter the housewife used to depend almost entirely on the huge bag of oatmeal kept in one corner of the kitchen and a barrel of salt herrings in another, to keep her family well fed. Even today, cooking over an open peat fire with cauldron and girdle is not a rarity.

Before the arrival of the travelling baker's van, and before other enterprising shop-keepers put their wares on wheels, the Highland housewife had little to offer but porridge, oatcakes, soup, fresh or smoked fish, and vegetables grown in the garden; the hardy kail or cabbage, and the beloved tatties and neeps – potatoes and swedes.

But travel as far south as Dundee, and the milder Lowlands, or to the great twin cities of Edinburgh on the East and Glasgow on the West coasts of Scotland, and there's a splendid selection of baked goods and sweetmeats to delight you. The Lowland housewife has plenty of flour, a good oven, and a skilled hand with yeasted breads, rolls and cakes.

This beautiful land of mountains, lochs and castles is often dominated by stormy skies.

Porridge

Crofters' wives often left their porridge pots at the back of the range all night to cook. With a big family to feed it was the custom to scrub out a kitchen drawer once a week, make a pot full of porridge and pour it into the drawer so that the children could cut cold slices of it whenever they liked. Almost all Scots love porridge and agree that salt should be added to the water before the oatmeal to bring out the nutty flavour, and that hot sweet (fresh) milk is better than cold milk or cream to pour over it.

The traditional Scottish recipe uses medium oatmeal and takes a full half hour to cook. Bring 600 ml/1 pint water to the boil, add 1 teaspoon salt and sprinkle in 3 tablespoons oatmeal, or a modest handful, stirring constantly. The proper implement is a spurtle, a wooden stick as long as a large wooden spoon, with a handle carved in the shape of a thistle. Simmer the porridge for 30 minutes, stirring occasionally. When cooked, the porridge should be thick enough to hold the mark of the spurtle down to the base of the pan. Serve in wooden bowls sprinkled with salt. *Makes 4 servings. Illustrated overleaf.*

The gruel (preferred further south) made partly with milk and served liberally sprinkled with sugar, is called by Highlanders 'baby's porage'. Rolled oats which cook in a few minutes are rarely used in the North of Scotland.

There are other ways to cook porridge; soaking the oats overnight in water, or stirring to a paste with cold water before adding boiling water. It is then cooked for only 10 minutes.

Breakfast Crowdie

In the Highlands, breakfast time was once called crowdie time, and any kind of porridge eaten at breakfast was called a crowdie, although it had nothing to do with crowdie cheese.

A great treat, which also has nothing to do with cheese, is called Cream Crowdie, or Cranachan.

Cranachan

This is a luxury dish for special occasions. Nowadays it is often made with vanilla ice cream instead of whipped cream. To make it, soften the ice cream slightly, stir in the toasted oatmeal and serve immediately.

4 tablespoons coarse oatmeal
300 ml/½ pint whipping cream
¼ teaspoon vanilla essence
2 tablespoons castor sugar

Brown the oatmeal on a girdle or toast on a sheet of foil under the grill, shaking once or twice. Allow to cool. Whip the cream with the vanilla essence and sugar until thick but not stiff. Fold in almost all the toasted oatmeal and serve in small dishes sprinkled with the remaining oatmeal. *Makes 4 servings. Illustrated overleaf.*

Crowdie-Mowdie This delicious variation is really a pudding. The night before it is wanted for next day's midday meal, put a handful of oatmeal, ½ teaspoon salt and a breakfast cup of milk per person into a large stone jar or china pudding basin. Stir well, cover and let it stand all night. In the morning, set the covered jar or basin in a saucepan of water and steam it for 2–4 hours, according to the size of the pudding.

Crowdie

Throughout Scotland, crowdie means a homemade cheese, which is softer and creamier than cottage cheese. Crowdie produces a lot of whey, so here is a basic recipe for making Crowdie and one for Whey Oatcakes which uses up the whey.

1.15 litres/2 pints fresh milk (see note)
¼ teaspoon essence of rennet
little salt

Warm the milk to 22°C/72°F. Stir in the rennet and leave until set. Cut into cubes with a knife and leave to stand until the whey flows freely. Place the curds in a jelly bag or piece of muslin and allow to drain into a basin. (Reserve all the whey for the following recipe.) After about 2 hours, crumble the curds and add a little salt. Press into a pot. Serve with oatcakes or girdle scones. *Makes 3–4 servings.*

Note If using pasteurised milk you will need twice the quantity of rennet.

Whey Oatcakes

225 g/8 oz medium oatmeal
½ teaspoon salt
generous pinch of bicarbonate of soda
150 ml/¼ pint whey from making Crowdie
extra oatmeal to sprinkle

Combine the oatmeal, salt and bicarbonate of soda in a bowl. Heat the whey but do not allow it to boil. Pour into the oatmeal mixture and form into a firm paste. Turn on to a surface generously sprinkled with oatmeal and roll out thinly. Cut into small rounds, or into large rounds using a saucepan lid, then into farls (quarters). Arrange on an ungreased baking tray and bake in a moderately hot oven (200°C, 400°F, Gas Mark 6) for about 12 minutes. Lift carefully on to a cooling rack to harden. These are best served warm with butter. For extra crispness, oatcakes which have been allowed to get cold can be lightly toasted before serving. *Makes about 12.*

Atholl Brose

The name brose conjures up pictures in the mind of a delicacy. But in truth a Scottish brose is rarely ambrosial. It may simply be a savoury oatmeal porridge seasoned with pepper as well as salt, or made with the bree (stock) from cooking vegetables. Neep brose, made with the stock from cooking swedes, is a great favourite. A more formidable brose is a highly alcoholic drink made from fermented oatmeal. Mixed with whisky and honey, it soars to refined heights under the name Atholl Brose.

Here is a typical recipe, based on 'a braw handful' of oatmeal. Cover the oatmeal with water and leave to stand overnight. Strain off the liquid, measure and whisk together with the same quantity of runny honey. Pour in the same measured amount of whisky and stir until frothy. This concoction can be drunk immediately, or bottled, and will keep tightly corked for up to a month. Atholl Brose is usually drunk at a St. Andrew's Day feast. *Illustrated on pages 30–31.*

Heather Ale

A heady drink, though not as potent as Atholl Brose, is made with heather when the flowers are in full bloom. The recipe requires heather, hops, barm (beer froth), golden syrup, ginger and water. It takes several days to make this drink and it is still enjoyed in remote parts of the Highlands.

Cooking on a Girdle

In Scotland, certainly among country people if not in towns, oatmeal has always been easier to come by than flour and the girdle over an open fire was more frequently used than an oven. Even now, Scottish housewives often bake on a girdle, or use as a substitute a heavy frying pan or the largest smooth hotplate of an electric cooker. Yeasted bread is still rarely seen in country districts, because distances are too great and the population too sparse for village bakers to distribute it. The baker's van might have to trundle over twenty miles of rocky roads to visit as few as five lonely crofts. And housewives can always knock up a batch of oatcakes or bannocks without fresh yeast – dried yeast is, after all, a relative newcomer to the kitchen.

Oatcakes

The original oatcake was a spartan mixture of oatmeal and cold water, not necessarily cooked at all. Until quite recently, fishermen chasing the elusive herring shoals would dip a handful of oatmeal over the side of the boat into the sea and when it was thoroughly moistened, press it into a cake and eat it. The basic recipe for oatcakes that most Scots prefer is still the time-honoured one their ancestors used to bake on the flat hearthstone of the fire.

Traditional Oatcakes

If whey is not available it is necessary to substitute hot water and a little melted fat.

225 g/8 oz medium oatmeal
¼ teaspoon salt
¼ teaspoon bicarbonate of soda
1 tablespoon melted butter or bacon fat
sufficient hot water to give a stiff paste

Make the oatcakes by the same method as given for Whey Oatcakes (see above). Keep the ball of paste and the working surface well sprinkled with oatmeal to prevent sticking while rolling out. Cut into rounds with a 6-cm/2½-inch cutter and cook on a hot greased girdle until the edges curl. *Makes 18. Illustrated overleaf.*

Bannocks

Like oatcakes, bannocks are traditionally cooked on a girdle, but they are usually sweet and spiced, and made with flour or a mixture of flour and oatmeal or barley meal. A grander version, the Selkirk Bannock, is yeasted and mixed with dried fruit before baking in the oven. The best-loved basic recipe for bannocks gives a pouring mixture which produces a kind of drop scone.

Traditional Bannocks

100 g/4 oz plain flour
generous pinch of ground cinnamon
generous pinch of salt
3 eggs
1 tablespoon sugar
milk to mix

Sift together the flour, cinnamon and salt. Whisk the eggs lightly with the sugar and stir into the flour mixture with just enough milk to give a pouring consistency. Beat well until bubbles form. Grease and heat a girdle. Pour tablespoons of the mixture on to it, tilting to spread the mixture thinly. As soon as the bannocks are golden brown underneath, flip them over and brown on the other side. Cool on a wire rack. Serve with butter and heather honey. *Makes about 12.*

Below
Morning Rolls and Baps

Barley Bannocks

175 g/6 oz plain flour
100 g/4 oz barley meal
1 teaspoon cream of tartar
generous pinch of salt
25 g/1 oz lard, melted
sour milk or buttermilk to mix

Mix all the dry ingredients together. Pour in the melted fat, add enough milk to make a soft dough, roll out and tear off pieces. Pat into thin rounds and bake on a hot greased girdle for 3 minutes on each side. *Makes about 12.*

Right
In Scotland, oatmeal is used in all manner of sweet and savoury dishes, not least being that staple breakfast food, porridge. From left: Porridge, Skirlie, Traditional Oatcakes, and Cranachan, plus on the table a selection of Scottish cheeses and heather honey.

Skirlie

The old name for this savoury oatmeal mixture was skirl-in-the-pan and refers to the noise it makes while cooking. Skirlie may be used as a stuffing for chicken or, with a little stock added, it is served as a main dish with chappit tatties (mashed potatoes). Children also call this dish 'Glory' and it is a favourite with them in winter when they come home from school.

To make it, warm 100 g/4 oz shredded suet in a heavy frying pan until the fat runs, or melt the same amount of good meat dripping. Add a finely chopped medium onion, or a few chopped shallots, and stir over moderate heat until the onion is golden. Add 225 g/8 oz oatmeal with salt and pepper to tase and cook until soft, stirring. *Makes 4 servings. Illustrated on preceding pages.*

Snap and Rattle

Small children often went to bed on a supper made by toasting oatcakes and serving them well broken up and soaked in hot milk. With sugar sprinkled on and a knot (knob) of butter, it is surprisingly good. When there were plenty of oatcakes left over from the previous day, the whole family might have this dish for breakfast.

Morning Rolls and Baps

In southern Scotland a selection of yeasted bread rolls is often served at breakfast as well as porridge. Baps are the great favourites.

A plain white bread dough is used (see page 83), but if the bread is made early in the morning to be eaten at breakfast, then, in order to obtain a quick rise, the proportion of yeast is increased, using 25 g/1 oz to each 450 g/1 lb flour.

The dough is usually shaped into one large round bap and a number of small rolls. This soft-crusted bread is brushed with milk and sprinkled with flour before baking so that the golden surface is seen through a delicate dusting of white. *Illustrated on page 18.*

Butteries

A well-risen plain white bread dough (see page 83) is rolled out, dotted with a mixture of butter and lard, sealed and rolled out again several times, like making puff pastry. The resulting rolls are very rich and should be eaten warm otherwise they taste rather greasy.

Soups

Soups are among the simplest dishes to cook by the ancient method, in a cauldron over an open fire. Scotland excels in the variety of her broths and soups, including some surprisingly delicate ones made with chicken, a result of the strong influence of French cuisine derived from the 'Auld Alliance'. On the other hand, thrifty Scottish housewives stretch meat stock with pulses and cereals to make a vegetable soup called Tattie Drottle, first cousin of Tattie Hushie (see page 60); and an even more economical soup based on mixing the water from cooking various vegetables called Ca'canny Soup.

Scotch Broth

The old method of cooking whatever meat and vegetables were available together with a cereal to make it more filling, is seen at its traditional best in the world-renowned Scotch Broth. Sometimes a little beef is substituted for part of the mutton.

50 g/2 oz dried peas
675 g/1½ lb neck of mutton
50 g/2 oz pearl barley
2 litres/3½ pints water
salt and pepper
2 leeks, trimmed
1 large onion, chopped
1 large carrot, diced
1 medium swede, diced
1 tablespoon chopped parsley

Cover the dried peas with cold water and leave to soak overnight. Drain well. Trim off as much of the fat from the meat as possible, cut into four pieces and place in a large saucepan with the drained peas, pearl barley and water. Bring to the boil, skim, then season with salt and pepper and simmer for 30 minutes. Meanwhile, slice the leeks and rinse well. Add to the pan with the onion, carrot and swede. Cover and cook gently for 2 hours. Check the seasoning. Remove the meat and serve separately, or cut some of it into cubes and return to the soup. Serve very hot sprinkled with parsley. *Makes 6 servings. Illustrated overleaf.*

Cock-a-Leekie

Sir Walter Scott put the following poetic words into the mouth of King James VI of Scotland and I of England. 'My lords and lieges, let us all to dinner for the cockie-leekie is a-cooling.' Rather a tongue twister for a king reputed to suffer from a speech impediment, but if correctly made the soup itself is almost worthy of a poem. Most classic recipes include the prunes but oddly enough Scotland's Mrs Beeton, Mistress Meg Dods, omits them from hers.

1 small boiling fowl
4–6 leeks, trimmed
1 large carrot, sliced
100 g/4 oz bacon, diced
½ teaspoon ground allspice
1 bouquet garni
salt and pepper
6 prunes, soaked overnight
2 tablespoons long-grain rice

Place the bird in a large saucepan and cover with water. Slice the leeks finely, rinse well and add to the pan with the carrot, bacon, allspice, bouquet garni and seasoning to taste. Bring to the boil, cover and simmer for 3 hours, skimming occasionally. Add the prunes and rice to the pan and cook for a further 30 minutes. Take out the fowl and serve as the main course. (If preferred, part of the meat may be diced and returned to the pan.) Remove the prunes, stone them and return to the soup. Adjust the seasoning and serve very hot. *Makes 6 servings.* *Illustrated overleaf.*

Lorraine Soup

Opinion differs as to the origin of this recipe – it might have been named in honour of James V's wife, Mary of Guise and Lorraine, or simply be a derivation from the old French 'à la reine'. No one knows for certain but the recipe is quite exquisite.

75 g/3 oz cooked white chicken meat
1 hard-boiled egg yolk
25 g/1 oz fresh white breadcrumbs
25 g/1 oz butter
2 tablespoons flour
1.15 litres/2 pints chicken stock
finely grated rind of 1 lemon
¼ teaspoon freshly grated nutmeg
salt and pepper
75 g/3 oz ground almonds
150 ml/¼ pint single cream
2 tablespoons chopped parsley

Mince together the chicken, egg yolk and breadcrumbs. Melt the butter in a large saucepan, stir in the flour. Gradually add the stock and bring to the boil, stirring constantly. Add the chicken mixture, lemon rind and nutmeg. Season to taste, cover and simmer for 15 minutes. Stir in the ground almonds, cream and parsley. Taste and adjust for seasoning. Reheat but do not allow to boil. Serve at once *Makes 6 servings.* *Illustrated overleaf.*

Feather Fowlie

This is another soup with an intriguing name, probably a corruption of the French, as the Scots found it difficult to pronounce the proper title 'Velouté de Volaille'. The custom of soaking the chicken portions can probably be dispensed with, although it is always mentioned in the authentic old recipes for this soup. The result may not be quite as rich, but it is still excellent if two chicken wing portions only are used.

1 small chicken, jointed
50 g/2 oz lean ham
1 stick celery, chopped
1 medium onion, sliced
1 blade of mace or ¼ teaspoon ground mace
1 sprig of thyme
1 sprig of parsley
1.75 litres/3 pints water
salt and pepper
1 tablespoon chopped parsley
3 egg yolks
3 tablespoons single cream

Soak the chicken portions in salted water for 1 hour. Drain, rinse and place in a large saucepan with the ham, celery, onion, mace, thyme and parsley. Pour over the water and add seasoning to taste. Bring to the boil and simmer for about 1½ hours. Strain the stock into a clean saucepan and allow to cool. Skim off any fat. Bring to the boil again and add the chopped parsley. Take the white meat from the chicken, mince or chop it finely and stir into the soup. Beat together the egg yolks and cream, stir in a little of the hot soup then return this mixture to the saucepan and reheat without boiling, stirring constantly. Adjust seasoning. *Makes 6 servings.*

Bawd Bree

Bawd is the Scottish name for a hare, and bree means soup or stock, although clear soups are also called broths. Partan Bree (crab soup) is another favourite, made with cream.

1 hare
1.4 litres/2½ pints cold water
salt and freshly ground black pepper
50 g/2 oz swede, diced
50 g/2 oz carrots, diced
3 peppercorns
2 cloves
50 g/2 oz oatmeal
pinch of sugar
2 tablespoons port

Skin and joint the hare and reserve any blood. Save the back legs and some of the fleshy part of the back for jugged or roast hare. Put the remaining joints into a saucepan with the water, salt and vegetables. Bring to the boil, add the peppercorns and cloves, cover and simmer gently for 3–4 hours, until the meat is tender. Remove the joints of hare, cut the meat from the bones. Add the meat to the soup and discard the bones. Stir in the oatmeal and sugar and adjust seasoning. Bring to the boil, stirring. Meanwhile, mix the blood with an equal quantity of cold water. Remove the saucepan from the heat and add the blood liquid and the port, stirring all the time. Reheat gently, stirring, but do not allow to boil. *Makes 6 servings. Illustrated left.*

Left
When it's raining outdoors, what more welcome than a plate of warm and nourishing soup? These four from Scotland are full of good things. From left: Bawd Bree, Cock-a-Leekie, Scotch Broth, and in the tureen, Lorraine Soup, an exquisite combination of chicken, almonds and cream.
Below
Herrings in Oatmeal

Fish

The Scots are great fish eaters and produce many delicacies in the way of smoked fish; these are exported as well as enjoyed at home. Kippers need no introduction at one end of the social scale, and smoked salmon at the other. Also appreciated in warmer climes is the smoked haddock, often called by the old name of Finnan Haddie; Finnan is a corruption of Findon, the name of the town where smoking the fish was once the only industry. The haddock are caught fairly large, split and then cured to a rich golden yellow. Delicious Arbroath Smokies are also a local speciality; these are small whole fishes smoked until copper in colour.

Herrings

These are popularly known all around the coast of Scotland as silver darlings. Being so readily available in a country where one is never far from the sea, herrings have always been used in many different ways; potted, pickled for short-term keeping, and salted for long-term preservation. Of course, they are also smoked to make kippers. Fried herrings in Scotland are served with vinegar and oatcakes.

Herrings in Oatmeal

4 herrings, cleaned
salt and pepper
100 g/4 oz coarse oatmeal
100 g/4 oz dripping or butter

Slash the herrings three times on each side. Season well inside and out and coat in oatmeal. Melt the dripping and use to fry the herrings for about 15 minutes, turning once carefully. Drain well.

Alternatively, split the herrings, pull out the back bone then flatten them, season on both sides and coat in oatmeal. Fried like this, the herrings require only 5 minutes each side. *Makes 4 servings. Illustrated below.*

Steamed Herring

A Reverend Alexander Stewart, writing in 1883, described visiting a croft and enjoying the following meal. The 'gude wife' poured off the water from her cauldron of cooked potatoes, shortened the chain which kept it suspended over the fire so the potatoes would not burn, and arranged some fresh gutted herrings over the potatoes. She laid a clean cloth over the fish and then put on a lid. After 15 minutes, judging the fish to be cooked from the sound of bubbling inside the pot, she removed the lid. The cauldron was placed in the middle of the floor, the family sat round on low stools, and dipped into the pot, pulling out a handful of fish or a hot potato, until the feast was consumed. This was certainly the way food was eaten except in the grandest houses.

Tweed Kettle

Everyone knows this odd sounding recipe is in fact a delicacy made with fresh salmon, not always come by legally or in season. The old title is still used today; just as the vessel in which the fish is cooked is still called a fish kettle and not a saucepan.

450 g/1 lb fresh salmon
salt and pepper
pinch of ground mace
1 shallot, chopped or 1 tablespoon chopped chives
3 tablespoons wine vinegar
2 tablespoons chopped parsley

Place the salmon in a fish kettle or saucepan and cover with cold water. Bring to the boil and cook gently for 5 minutes only. Drain and reserve 150 ml/¼ pint of the cooking liquid. Remove the skin and all bones from the salmon. Cut into large pieces and return to the same pan with seasoning to taste, the mace, shallot, reserved liquid and wine vinegar. Bring to the boil, cover and simmer for about 30 minutes, until the salmon is cooked. Place all in a heated serving dish and sprinkle with the parsley. *Makes 4 servings.*

Cabbie Claw

The name is probably a corruption of the French for codling 'cabillaud', but the title has another ingenious explanation. Visitors to a great house once travelled by coach and horses. The cabbie (coachman) would eat with the staff in the kitchen. When there was lobster or crab on the menu in the dining room, the staff were given Cabbie Claw. After a dram of whisky the coachman probably did not notice the difference, as flaked cod sprinkled with egg yolk and paprika can look like meat from the claw of a crab or lobster.

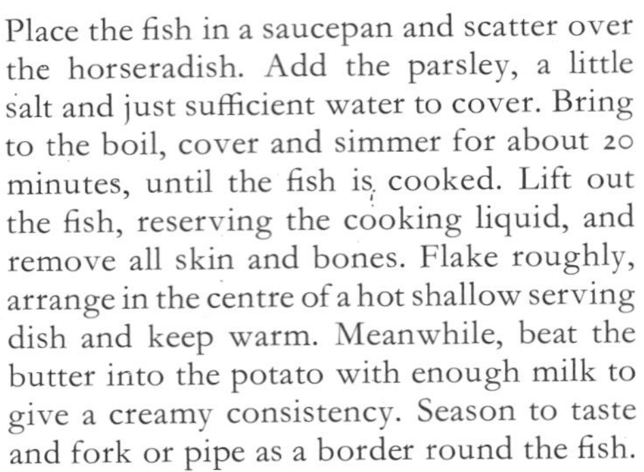

450 g/1 lb cod fillet
1 teaspoon grated horseradish
1 large sprig of parsley
salt and pepper
25 g/1 oz butter
450 g/1 lb hot mashed potato
little milk
hot paprika or cayenne pepper

Sauce

25 g/1 oz butter
25 g/1 oz flour
300 ml/½ pint milk
1 egg, hard-boiled

Place the fish in a saucepan and scatter over the horseradish. Add the parsley, a little salt and just sufficient water to cover. Bring to the boil, cover and simmer for about 20 minutes, until the fish is cooked. Lift out the fish, reserving the cooking liquid, and remove all skin and bones. Flake roughly, arrange in the centre of a hot shallow serving dish and keep warm. Meanwhile, beat the butter into the potato with enough milk to give a creamy consistency. Season to taste and fork or pipe as a border round the fish.

To make the sauce, melt the butter, stir in the flour and cook for 1 minute. Gradually add the milk and 150 ml/¼ pint strained liquid from cooking the fish. Bring to the boil, stirring all the time, until the sauce is smooth and thickened. Chop the hard-boiled egg white and stir into the sauce with seasoning to taste. Spoon over the fish. Press the yolk of the egg through a sieve over the sauce and sprinkle with paprika or cayenne. *Makes 4 servings.*

Cullen Skink

A mystifying name for a dish reminiscent of the American chowder. In the old Scots tongue cullen means fish and skink means stew.

225 g/8 oz potato, diced
1 large onion, chopped
about 450 ml/¾ pint milk
450 g/1 lb smoked haddock fillet
salt and pepper
25 g/1 oz butter

Place the potato, onion and milk in a saucepan. Cook gently for about 20 minutes, until the vegetables are very soft. Cut the fish into chunks, add to the pan, cover and simmer for a further 20 minutes, until cooked. Season to taste and stir in the butter just before serving. *Makes 4 servings.*

Meat

The wonderful beef which Scotland exports, including the renowned Aberdeen Angus, is often too expensive to be used in homely recipes. Mutton is still easier to get in Scotland than the lamb which is so readily available further south.

Haggis

Here is Scottish cooking at its most inventive and thrifty. In a country devoted to sheep farming it is hardly surprising that a way has been found to turn meat that would otherwise be wasted into a delicious savoury dish. Robert Burns in his ode 'To a Haggis' describes it as 'Great chieftain o' the puddin'-race'.

1 sheep's stomach bag plus the pluck
(lights, liver and heart)
450 g/1 lb lean mutton
175 g/6 oz fine oatmeal
225 g/8 oz shredded suet
2 large onions, chopped
salt and pepper
about 150 ml/¼ pint beef stock

Soak the stomach bag in salted water overnight. Place the pluck (lights, liver and heart) in a saucepan with the windpipe hanging over the edge. Cover with water and boil for 1½ hours. Impurities will pass out through the windpipe and it is advisable to place a basin under it to catch any drips. Drain well and cool. Remove the windpipe and any gristle or skin.

Mince the liver and heart with the mutton. (Add some of the lights before mincing if you wish.) Toast the oatmeal gently until pale golden brown and crisp. Combine with the minced mixture, suet and onion. Season well and add sufficient stock to moisten well. Pack into the stomach bag, filling it just over half-full as the stuffing will swell during cooking. Sew up the bag tightly or secure each end with string. Put an upturned plate in the base of a saucepan of boiling water, stand the haggis on this and bring back to the boil. Prick the haggis all over with a large needle to avoid bursting and boil steadily for 3–4 hours. *Makes 6–8 servings. Illustrated overleaf.*

Note If making two smaller haggis (as illustrated), attach them with a length of string to a wooden rod. Gently lower into the pan of boiling water and rest the wooden rod on the top of the pan. This way the haggis cook more evenly.

Pan Haggis

350 g/12 oz lamb's liver
2 medium onions, chopped
175 g/6 oz shredded suet
75 g/3 oz medium oatmeal
salt and pepper

Place the liver in a saucepan with the onion. Cover with cold water and cook gently for about 30 minutes. Strain off the liquid and reserve. When the liver is cold, mince it finely and place in a saucepan with the onion, suet and oatmeal. Season well and add sufficient of the reserved stock to make it moist but not watery. Simmer for about 1½ hours, stirring occasionally and adding a little more liquid if necessary. Alternatively, the mixture can be placed in a greased pudding basin and steamed for about 2 hours. *Makes 4 servings.*

Forfar Bridies

450 g/1 lb rump steak or topside
75 g/3 oz shredded suet
salt and pepper
little beef stock
350 g/12 oz shortcrust pastry
(made with 350 g/12 oz flour, etc.)
1 egg, beaten

Unless the meat is known to be tender, beat it out thinly with a meat mallet or rolling pin. Cut into narrow strips and place in a basin with the suet. Season well and add a little stock to moisten the mixture. Roll out the pastry and cut into four rounds, each the size of a tea plate. Divide the filling between the rounds, keeping it on one side of the pastry. Lift the uncovered pastry over the filling, brush the edges with beaten egg and seal well together, to make half-moon shaped pasties. Flute the edges and cut a small steam vent in the top of each one. Brush all over with beaten egg and place on a greased baking tray. Bake in a moderate oven (180°C, 350°F, Gas Mark 4) for about 55 minutes, until rich golden brown. *Makes 4.*

To a Haggis

Fair fa' your honest sonsie face,
Great chieftain o' the puddin'-race!
Aboon them a' ye tak your place,
Painch, tripe, or thairm:
Weel are ye wordy of a grace
As lang's my arm.

Robert Burns

The haggis. In Scotland, no Burns Night Supper would be complete without the main dish, a haggis, being solemnly piped into the dining room.

Mince Collops with Sippets

These collops (shortened from the French 'escalopes') are made with beef, but are equally well known made with venison or mutton. Sometimes sufficient oatmeal is added to make the mixture firm enough to form into patties for frying. The sippets are like croûtons but toasted or baked on the girdle until almost like rusks. Slices of cooked meat heated in gravy are also called collops.

25 g/1 oz dripping
1 medium onion, chopped
450 g/1 lb minced beef or mutton
300 ml/½ pint beef stock
salt and pepper
50 g/2 oz medium oatmeal
2 slices bread

Melt the dripping and use to fry the onion until soft. Add the minced beef and fry, stirring, until the mixture is brown and crumbly. Break up any lumps. Add the stock and season to taste. Cook gently for about 20 minutes. Stir in the oatmeal and continue to cook for a further 30 minutes. Meanwhile, make the sippets. Toast the bread slices, trim and cut into triangles. Serve with the collops. *Makes 4 servings.*

Sassermaet

450 g/1 lb minced beef
225 g/8 oz shredded suet
½ teaspoon freshly grated nutmeg
½ teaspoon ground cloves
1½ teaspoons ground mixed spice
1½ teaspoons ground ginger
1 teaspoon ground allspice
1 teaspoon sugar
1 egg, beaten
salt and freshly ground black pepper

Place the beef and suet in a basin and sprinkle over the spices and sugar. Add the beaten egg, season with salt and pepper and work into the meat until evenly blended. Divide into eight equal portions and with floured hands shape each into a round flat brunie (cake). Place in a large cold frying pan and fry gently for about 15 minutes on each side, until well browned. *Makes 4 servings.*

Note This mixture may be too heavily spiced for some tastes.

Baked Ayrshire Bacon

1.75 kg/4 lb joint of unsmoked bacon
40 g/1½ oz bacon fat
1 medium onion, chopped
100 g/4 oz medium oatmeal

Soak the bacon in cold water overnight. Drain and place in a saucepan with fresh cold water to cover. Bring to the boil, cover and simmer for 1¼ hours. Drain and strip off the rind if necessary. Place the joint in a roasting tin. Melt the bacon fat and use to fry the onion gently until soft. Stir in the oatmeal and spread this mixture over the fat surface of the bacon. Bake in a moderately hot oven (190°C, 375°F, Gas Mark 5) for 1 hour. If preferred, the joint can be rolled and tied and baked for 1½ hours. *Makes 8 servings.*

Inky-Pinky

4 button onions
300 ml/½ pint beef stock or thin gravy
450 g/1 lb cold roast beef
225 g/8 oz cooked carrots, sliced
1½ teaspoons vinegar
salt and pepper
1 tablespoon cornflour

Place the onions in a saucepan with the stock and cook gently for about 30 minutes. Trim the beef, removing any fat or skin and slice thinly. Add to the pan with the carrots and vinegar and season to taste. Reheat to boiling point. Moisten the cornflour with a little cold water, add to the pan and bring to the boil, stirring constantly. Cook for 2 minutes. Serve with toast sippets (see above). *Makes 4 servings.*

The Vegetable Patch

Of all root crops, the potato reigns supreme in Scotland. The cook knows her varieties, buys them by name and expects characteristic cooking quality and flavour from each. Potatoes figure as frequently as oatmeal in traditional main dishes, often along with another Scottish favourite, neeps. Turnips, or neeps, are not the globular white vegetables known by this name further south, but the sweeter, golden-fleshed swede. Potatoes were introduced from Ireland early in the Eighteenth Century, and since then, larger crofts have always had a 'tattie hoose' close by. This is dug out of the earth, roofed over, then thatched with turf to make a dark, dry storage house, and supplies are brought in to the kitchen once a week. Potatoes, either on their own or combined with other root vegetables, kail or cabbage, often made the main meal, or were served at every meal of the day.

Breakfast Tatties

Boil well-scrubbed potatoes with their skins on until tender. Strain, cool a little, peel and return to the pan over a low heat. Sprinkle on oatmeal and salt to taste, then mash the potatoes, heat through and serve out portions piping hot to be eaten with the morning's fresh milk, or with buttermilk.

Dinner Tatties

Boil potatoes as above, drain off water, shake dry, and empty into a large basin, or tip out on to the middle of the kitchen table. The family gathers round, each member takes a potato, peels it with the fingers (taking care not to burn them, since it is not usual to provide knife or fork) and dips the potato into a communal pot of melted butter.

Supper Tatties

These are prepared with other root vegetables, or with fresh fish if available. Some of the variations have delightful names which defy tracing to their origin. Here is just a selection. Only one recipe needs to be cooked in the oven.

Rumbledethumps

450 g/1 lb cabbage, shredded
450 g/1 lb potatoes, sliced
1 large onion, sliced (optional)
50 g/2 oz butter
salt and pepper
50 g/2 oz cheese, grated

Cook the cabbage and potatoes separately in boiling salted water until tender. Cook the onion, if used, with the potatoes. Drain, saving the stock for soup. Layer the cabbage, potatoes and onion in an ovenproof dish, dotting each layer with butter and adding salt and pepper to taste. Sprinkle cheese over the top and bake in a moderately hot oven (190°C, 375°F, Gas Mark 5) for about 25 minutes. *Makes 4 servings.*

Kailkenny

Mash equal quantities of boiled kail or cabbage and potatoes together. Beat in as much double cream as you can spare, at least 2 tablespoons per portion, season well with salt and freshly ground pepper and heat through.

Clapshot

This recipe is the traditional accompaniment to haggis, and is sometimes described as bashed tatties and neeps.

450 g/1 lb swede, diced
450 g/1 lb potatoes, diced
salt and pepper
50 g/2 oz butter or dripping
1 tablespoon chopped chives

Cook the vegetables together in just enough boiling salted water to cover, until tender. Drain, mash well until smooth and season to taste. Reheat, adding the butter and chives, and serve piping hot. *Makes 6 servings.*

Tatties and P'int

To make the inevitable potato dish more interesting, a sauce is sometimes made by soaking oatmeal in milk, straining off the milk and boiling this up with salt, pepper and mustard. This thin mustard sauce is poured over boiled potatoes, and when meat or fish are scarce, provides a tattie and p'int dinner; really nothing but potatoes and just a rueful finger to 'point' at the herring barrel or ham hanging from the rafters.

Above
Potato Scones

Potato Scones

50–100 g/2–4 oz plain flour
generous pinch of salt
milk to mix
450 g/1 lb mashed potato

Sift the flour with the salt. Knead sufficient flour and milk into the mashed potato to make a stiff dough. The amount will depend on the variety of potato used. Roll out very thinly on a floured board. Cut into rounds and prick with a fork. Bake on a hot greased girdle for 2–3 minutes, turn and cook for a further 2 minutes. Top with a knob of butter and serve at once, while still hot. *Makes about 10. Illustrated above.*

Stovies

Fry a layer of sliced onion in a little dripping in a large saucepan. Cover with a deep layer of sliced potatoes. Sprinkle with salt and pepper, cover closely and cook over a low heat for about 1 hour, depending on the depth of the layer of potatoes. It is important not to remove the lid and lose steam during cooking, or the potatoes may burn. When tender, turn the potatoes to bring the onion base up to the top, and serve at once.

Roasted Onions

Large onions are roasted near the fire, or in the ashes, in their skins. When soft if pricked with a fork, they are peeled and served with melted butter or bacon fat.

Right
Afore ye go . . . stay awhile to sample some of these tempting Scottish sweetmeats. From left: Scots Tablet, Edinburgh Rock, Caledonian Cream, Whim-Wham, and a drop of the hard stuff in Atholl Brose.

Sweet Things

The Lowlands and South of Scotland are famous for their rich and substantial cakes and biscuits which owe their splendour to the oven rather than the girdle.

Once the delicate morning rolls and baps are disposed of, one can look forward to more miracles of fine baking at the celebrated high tea, often the main meal of the day. Cakes on the whole are more usual in the South and the only national favourite is Black Bun. (Bun and bonn are traditional synonyms for cakes in Scotland.)

In contrast to this filling fare, the Scots also turn their hand to desserts and sweetmeats, as light and delicious as anyone could wish for.

Apple Flory

There are a number of pastry tarts which are called Flory or Florentine tarts and the origin is less obscure than one might suppose; much of the sophisticated French influence on Scottish cuisine, wielded by Mary, Queen of Scots, was introduced direct from the French court dominated by her young husband's formidable mother, Catherine de Medici of Florence. Probably the most authentic filling is one made with ground almonds, orange flower water, candied lemon peel and currants. There is another variation with prunes, lemon juice and port, but this version is probably the least extravagant to make today.

450 g/1 lb cooking apples
about 50 g/2 oz sugar
4 tablespoons water
¼ teaspoon ground cinnamon
finely grated rind of ½ lemon
450 g/1 lb prepared puff pastry
3 tablespoons marmalade
milk to brush

Peel, core and slice the apples and place in a saucepan with the sugar and water. Cook gently until reduced to a pulp. Mix in the cinnamon and lemon rind and add more sugar if necessary. Roll out the pastry thinly and use half to line a deep 20-cm/8-inch pie plate. Spoon in the apple mixture. Gently warm the marmalade to soften it then spread over the apple filling. Use the remaining pastry to make a lid for the pie, dampen the edges, seal well together and flute them. Roll out the trimmings and use to make pastry leaves and flowers to decorate the pie. Brush all over with milk and bake in a hot oven (220°C, 425°F, Gas Mark 7) for 10 minutes, then reduce to moderately hot (190°C, 375°F, Gas Mark 5) for a further 20–25 minutes, until well risen and golden brown. Serve warm with cream. *Makes 4–6 servings.*

Caledonian Cream

The Latin name for Scotland was Caledonia, hence the title of this recipe, understandably a favourite with university dons of Edinburgh, Stirling, Glasgow and St. Andrews. No Scottish crofter could have afforded it. Meg Dods has a version which suggests that this is a Celtic syllabub. A modern version reduces the amount of marmalade but replaces the brandy with a mixture of Drambuie and Cointreau. However you do it, the result is very, very rich.

175 g/6 oz Dundee marmalade
175 g/6 oz castor sugar
juice of 3 lemons
150 ml/¼ pint brandy
900 ml/1½ pints double cream

Mince the marmalade finely. Dissolve the sugar in the lemon juice and brandy and stir in the marmalade. Half-whip the cream and gradually whisk in the marmalade mixture. *Makes 8 servings. Illustrated on preceding pages.*

Whim-Wham

Almost a trifle and chiefly useful because it could be put together at the last moment, in fact at the hostess's whim.

900 ml/1½ pints double cream
150 ml/¼ pint sweet white wine
75 g/3 oz castor sugar
finely grated rind of 1 lemon
12 soft sponge fingers
6 tablespoons redcurrant jelly
1 tablespoon chopped candied lemon peel

Whip the cream with the wine and sugar until it just holds the trace of the whisk. Add the lemon rind and whisk until thick. Spread the sponge fingers with the redcurrant jelly and place in the base of a shallow glass dish. Cover with the cream mixture and sprinkle the candied peel over the top. *Makes 8 servings. Illustrated on preceding pages.*

Edinburgh Rock

This famous sweetmeat is very different from the chewy confection known as rock in the South. The texture is rather dry and powdery.

To make it, dissolve granulated sugar in the proportion of 450 g/1 lb to 300 ml/½ pint water. Add the colouring and flavouring and when it comes to the boil add a pinch of cream of tartar. Let it boil to the hard ball stage (120°C, 250°F). Remove from the heat and pour on to an oiled work surface or large clean upturned tray. Allow the mass to cool until it begins to set then start turning the edges towards the centre with an oiled knife. When cool enough to handle, sprinkle it with sifted icing sugar, lift it and pull with your hands, keeping it straight. When it has formed a long matt rope, cut into pieces with kitchen scissors. Lay on a wooden board dusted with more icing sugar and leave to harden for 24 hours.

The traditional colours and flavourings are as follows: white – vanilla, pink – raspberry, biscuit – ginger, yellow or orange – orange. *Illustrated on preceding pages.*

Scots Tablet

250 ml/8 fl oz single cream
100 g/4 oz butter
1 kg/2 lb granulated sugar
½ teaspoon vanilla essence

Place the cream, butter and sugar in a heavy saucepan and heat gently until the sugar has completely dissolved. Bring to the boil and continue boiling without stirring until the mixture reaches a temperature of 115°C/240°F, or until a little dropped into cold water forms a soft ball. Cool slightly then add the vanilla essence and beat with a wooden spoon until the mixture becomes dull and begins to thicken and grain. Pour into a buttered 20-cm/8-inch square tin. Cut into squares when set but still warm. *Makes about 1 kg/2¼ lb.* *Illustrated on preceding pages.*

Marmalade

Dundee marmalade is world famous and indeed Scotland is looked upon generally as the origin of the recipe which uses Seville oranges for this delicious preserve. The word marmalade means, in fact, a jam (not necessarily made with citrus fruit), both in French and other languages, so that is probably the origin. Although the bitter orange which gives marmalade its unique flavour today was not used then, it is said that the confection was invented by Queen Mary's French cook when she was ill and refusing to eat – hence the name 'Marie Malade'. Marmalade was made with quinces long before bitter oranges were available and it was probably this blander version which tempted the royal invalid's appetite.

Raspberry Cheese

raspberries
450 g/1 lb castor sugar to
each 450 g/1 lb pulp

Press the raspberries through a sieve to remove the pips. Weigh the raspberry pulp and place in a preserving pan with an equal quantity of sugar. Heat gently until the sugar has dissolved then bring to the boil. Keep over moderate heat, boiling gently, until the mixture becomes thick. Stir frequently to make sure it does not stick. The cheese is the right consistency when a wooden spoon drawn through the mixture leaves a clear division and the bottom of the pan is visible. Press into small oiled moulds or jars and smooth the top. Cover and seal as for jam. Keep the cheeses in a cool dark place for at least 3 months before using to allow them to mature. Turn out and slice at the table. Serve to accompany hot or cold meat, poultry and game.

Ayrshire Shortbread

The term shortbread means a kind of cake with shortening in it. We still say shortcrust for pastry with fat rubbed into flour. There are many varieties of shortbread; this one is rolled out fairly thickly then cut into fingers or rounds.

100 g/4 oz rice flour
350 g/12 oz plain flour
¼ teaspoon salt
225 g/8 oz butter
175 g/6 oz castor sugar
2 egg yolks
4 tablespoons milk
castor sugar to sprinkle

Sift the flours and salt into a bowl and rub in the butter. Stir in the sugar, egg yolks and milk and form into a firm paste. Knead lightly on a floured surface. Press the mixture into a greased Swiss roll tin, level the surface and prick all over with a fork. Mark into fingers. Alternatively, roll out thickly, cut into rounds and place on a greased baking tray. Bake in a moderate oven (180°C, 350°F, Gas Mark 4), about 50 minutes for the tin and 20 minutes if in separate rounds. Allow to cool and harden before removing from the tin. Sprinkle with castor sugar to serve. *Illustrated right.*

Petticoat Tails

There are two schools of thought on the way this shortbread came to be named. The first claims that it is a corruption of the French 'petites gatelles', meaning small cakes. The second is that the shapes resemble the panels of a stiffened petticoat, which was worn rather like a hoop to hold out a lady's skirt. In the Shetland and Orkney islands, caraway seeds are added to a similar shortbread called Bride's Bonn, which is eaten at wedding feasts.

225 g/8 oz plain flour
pinch of salt
40 g/$1\frac{1}{2}$ oz castor sugar
2 tablespoons milk
100 g/4 oz butter
castor sugar to sprinkle

Sift the flour and salt into a bowl and stir in the sugar. Heat the milk and butter together until the fat melts. Pour into the flour mixture and work with the hand to form a smooth paste. Turn on to a floured surface and knead lightly. Roll out and cut into a round about 20 cm/8 inches in diameter then place on a baking tray lined with greaseproof paper or non-stick vegetable parchment. Cut out a round 5 cm/2 inches in diameter from the centre, then mark into eight portions from the outer edge to the centre ring. Bake in a moderate oven (160°C, 325°F, Gas Mark 3) for 30–40 minutes, until pale golden. Bake the cut out biscuit at the same time. Cool on a wire rack and when crisp sprinkle with castor sugar. *Illustrated left.*

It's teatime in Scotland – and what an abundance of riches. Not without reason are the Scots famed for their toothsome cakes and shortbreads. From left: Pitcaithly Bannock, Petticoat Tails, Black Bun, Ayrshire Shortbread, Dundee Cake and Selkirk Bannock.

Black Bun

This is a rather awesome confection, very heavy, dark and spicy. It can be kept for up to a year although it is extremely indigestible at any time. Robert Louis Stevenson called it 'a black substance inimical to life'. It is the traditional cake for Hogmanay or New Year's Day, although it was formerly eaten on Twelfth Night, in early January.

450 g/1 lb plain flour
pinch of salt
½ teaspoon baking powder
200 g/7 oz butter
beaten egg to brush
castor sugar to sprinkle
Filling
175 g/6 oz plain flour
2 teaspoons ground allspice
generous pinch of salt
½ teaspoon freshly ground black pepper
1 teaspoon ground cinnamon
1 teaspoon ground mixed spice
½ teaspoon cream of tartar
½ teaspoon baking powder
75 g/3 oz soft brown sugar
350 g/12 oz seedless raisins
450 g/1 lb currants
50 g/2 oz flaked almonds
50 g/2 oz chopped mixed peel
1 egg
2 tablespoons brandy or rum
3 tablespoons milk

First make the pastry. Sift the flour, salt and baking powder into a bowl and rub in the butter. Add just sufficient cold water to make a stiff paste and knead lightly. Roll out two-thirds of the pastry on a floured surface and use to line a greased 20-cm/8-inch cake tin or a 1-kg/2-lb loaf tin.

Now make the filling. Sift the flour with the allspice, salt, pepper, cinnamon, mixed spice, cream of tartar and baking powder. Stir in the sugar, fruit, nuts and peel. Add the egg, brandy and milk to moisten the mixture. Pack into the pastry case and smooth the top. Roll out remaining pastry and use to make a lid. Dampen the edges and seal well together. Prick all over with a fork and with a skewer prick four times right through to the base of tin. Brush with beaten egg and bake in a moderate oven (160°C, 325°F, Gas Mark 3) for 2 hours, then reduce to 150°C, 300°F, Gas Mark 2 and bake for about a further 1 hour. The bun is cooked when a thin skewer inserted carefully through the top crust into the filling comes out clean. Cool and store in an airtight tin for at least 2 weeks before cutting. Sprinkle with castor sugar to serve. *Illustrated on preceding pages.*

Selkirk Bannock

Queen Victoria caused a sensation when she visited Sir Walter Scott's granddaughter and refused the entire elegant menu prepared for her, accepting only a portion of Selkirk Bannock from which she made her meal.

675 g/1½ lb plain flour
½ teaspoon salt
100 g/4 oz butter
300 ml/½ pint milk
25 g/1 oz fresh yeast
about 100 g/4 oz castor sugar
50 g/2 oz currants
225 g/8 oz sultanas or seedless raisins
50 g/2 oz chopped mixed peel
sugar and milk to glaze

Sift the flour and salt into a bowl and make a well. Melt the butter and add the milk. Warm to blood heat. Cream the yeast with 1 teaspoon sugar and stir in the milk mixture. Pour into the flour well and sprinkle a little flour over the top to cover. Leave in a warm place for 30 minutes, until frothy. Stir the liquid into the flour to make a soft dough. Knead well on a floured surface until smooth and elastic. Grease the bowl, return the dough to it, cover and leave in a warm place until double in size. Turn out on a floured surface and work in the fruit, peel and sugar. Knead for 5 minutes and shape into a large flat round. Place on a greased baking tray, cover and prove in a warm place for about 30 minutes. Dissolve 1 teaspoon sugar in 1 tablespoon warm milk and brush over the bannock. Bake in a moderately hot oven (200°C, 400°F, Gas Mark 6) for about 25 minutes, until golden brown. *Illustrated on preceding pages.*

Pitcaithly Bannock

This recipe is never described as a shortbread, but it is in fact shorter in texture than a cake.

25 g/1 oz rice flour
175 g/6 oz plain flour
25 g/1 oz candied lemon peel, chopped
25 g/1 oz blanched almonds, chopped
100 g/4 oz butter
75 g/3 oz castor sugar
castor sugar to sprinkle

Sift the flours together and mix with the peel and almonds. Cream the butter and sugar together until light and fluffy. Gradually work in the flour mixture to make a firm paste. Form into a round about 18 cm/7 inches in diameter and place on a baking tray lined with greaseproof paper or non-stick vegetable parchment. Pinch the edges and score from the centre into eight triangular wedges. Bake in a moderate oven (160°C, 325°F, Gas Mark 3) for about 30 minutes, until pale golden brown. Cool on the baking tray until crisp and sprinkle the top with castor sugar. *Illustrated on preceding pages.*

Note Great patience is needed to work in all the flour, but resist the temptation to add any liquid. The flavour is improved by keeping for at least a week before cutting.

Crulla

Here the name has a Teutonic derivation unusual in a country where so many recipe names are taken from the French. The recipe must have come originally from Northern invaders.

50 g/2 oz butter
50 g/2 oz castor sugar
2 eggs
350 g/12 oz plain flour
½ teaspoon bicarbonate of soda
1 teaspoon cream of tartar
fat or oil to deep fry
castor sugar to sprinkle

Cream the butter and sugar together until light and fluffy and gradually beat in the eggs. Sift the flour with the bicarbonate of soda and cream of tartar and fold into the creamed mixture to make a soft scone-like dough. Roll out the dough thickly and cut into 15-cm/6-inch long narrow strips. Take three strips and plait them together. Repeat with the remaining strips. Deep fry a few at a time in hot fat or oil until golden brown. Drain well on absorbent paper and serve warm sprinkled with sugar. *Makes about 12.*

Dundee Cake

350 g/12 oz plain flour
¼ teaspoon salt
1 teaspoon baking powder
200 g/7 oz butter
200 g/7 oz castor sugar
4 eggs, beaten
225 g/8 oz sultanas
100 g/4 oz seedless raisins
100 g/4 oz currants
milk to mix
50 g/2 oz blanched almonds, split

Sift the flour with the salt and baking powder. Cream the butter with the sugar until pale and fluffy. Add the eggs a little at a time, beating well after each addition. Fold in the flour mixture then the dried fruit and sufficient milk to give a heavy dropping consistency. Grease a 20-cm/8-inch cake tin and line with a double layer of greaseproof paper. Tie a sheet of brown paper round the outside to extend slightly above the top of the tin. Pour in the cake mixture and level the top. Arrange the almonds in a neat pattern on top with the rounded sides upwards. Bake in a moderate oven (180°C, 350°F, Gas Mark 4) for 45 minutes then reduce heat to cool (150°C, 300°F, Gas Mark 2) for a further 1½–2 hours. Test by inserting a fine skewer into the centre of the cake which will come out clean if the cake is cooked. Leave in the tin until quite cold then strip off the lining paper and wrap closely in foil. Store in an airtight container for at least 2 weeks before cutting. *Illustrated on preceding pages.*

Abernethy Biscuits

225 g/8 oz plain flour
pinch of salt
1½ teaspoons baking powder
75 g/3 oz butter or lard
1 egg, beaten
75 g/3 oz castor sugar
about 2 tablespoons milk
¾ teaspoon caraway seeds

Sift the flour with the salt and baking powder into a bowl. Rub in the butter. Add the egg with the sugar and sufficient milk to make a stiff paste. Work in the caraway seeds.

Roll out on a lightly floured surface to a thickness of about 5 mm/¼ inch and cut into rounds. Place on greased baking trays and bake in a moderately hot oven (190°C, 375°F, Gas Mark 5) for 15 minutes. Cool slightly then transfer to a wire rack. *Makes about 12.*

IRELAND

Blessed with special advantages of fertile soil and temperate climate, the Emerald Isle has never been densely populated. Even today, half the produce of Irish agriculture is exported to other countries.

Roman invaders of Britain, and later Norman Conquerors, stopped short without reaching greedy hands towards this most westerly of our group of islands. Nor did returning crusaders from the Middle East introduce a wider range of foodstuffs as they did in England. Records which stretch far back in time show that the ancient Irish kingdoms were rich in dairy herds, oxen, pigs and sheep. From castle to humble cabin, few can have gone hungry. But since the sophisticated influence of other nations left no early imprint on the traditional cooking of the country, it remained primitive until the Elizabethan age, while the rest of Europe was already enjoying a vast variety of delicately spiced and seasoned foods.

Sir Walter Raleigh is said to have introduced a new crop in the Sixteenth Century which was to become the mainstay of the nation. The potato, not immediately accepted in England, soon found favour in Ireland. It was easy to cultivate and had one overwhelming advantage in troubled times: it matured under ground and Ireland's rich soil could safely guard this precious crop, while fields of grain were open to destruction from skirmishing marauders. If oatmeal is the basic food of the sturdy Scots, the same can be said of potatoes for the Irish, although many recipes would be familiar in both countries. The most famous dish to come out of this beautiful country is undoubtedly Irish Stew. Made in the authentic fashion it has more 'praties' in it than meat, but then almost all traditional Irish recipes include the beloved potatoes in their ingredients.

The Emerald Isle is rich in farm produce, for the livestock graze on lush green pastures.

Crubeen Pea Soup

Pig's trotters are known in Ireland as crubeens. Sometimes they are boiled and served quite simply, with thick slices of soda bread and a mug of Guinness to wash them down.

175 g/6 oz green or yellow dried peas
25 g/1 oz dried lentils
1 kg/2 lb pig's trotters
1 stick celery, chopped
1 medium onion, chopped
1.75 litres/3 pints bone stock
salt and pepper
175 g/6 oz boiling sausage, cooked

Soak the peas and lentils in cold water overnight. Slash the trotters. Put the drained peas and lentils, the celery, onion and trotters into a large saucepan and add the bone stock. Bring to the boil and skim. Cover and simmer for about 2 hours, until the trotters are tender. Remove the trotters and bone them. Liquidise the soup in a blender. Reheat the soup and adjust the seasoning. Add the meat from the trotters and the sliced sausage, heat through and serve piping hot. *Makes 4–6 servings.*

Ballymoney Oyster Soup

There is no better shellfish than that freshly caught in the Irish Sea.

2 large potatoes
36 fresh oysters
100 g/4 oz belly of pork, diced
900 ml/1½ pints boiling milk
1 bouquet garni
salt and pepper
40 g/1½ oz butter

Cook the potatoes in boiling water until just tender. Meanwhile, open the oysters and drain their liquor into a bowl. Fry the diced belly of pork over a gentle heat until just tender. Mash the cooked potatoes in a saucepan with the milk. Add the bouquet garni and season to taste. Bring to the boil, stirring. Add the pork with the oysters and their liquor and simmer for a few minutes. Adjust seasoning if necessary and stir in the butter. Serve immediately. *Makes 4 servings.*

Smoked and Flamed Herrings

Red herrings are first salted and then smoked to a fiercesome red dryness. They are purposely served rather salty to work up a good thirst.

4 smoked red herrings
50 g/2 oz butter
2 tablespoons Irish whiskey

Put the herrings into a saucepan, cover with boiling water and simmer for 3–5 minutes, depending upon their size. Lift them out, split lengthways and remove the heads, bones and skin. Melt the butter in a frying pan and use to fry the herring fillets for a few minutes. Arrange them in a shallow flameproof serving dish. Carefully heat the whiskey in a small saucepan. At the table, pour the warm whiskey over the herring fillets and ignite. *Makes 4 servings.*

Grilled Red Herrings

Soak the herrings in boiling water for a few minutes or, if preferred, in cold beer. Drain, and grill them whole, turning once, until the flesh parts easily from the bone when tested with a fork. Serve sprinkled with cayenne pepper on hot buttered toast or on a bed of mashed potato.

Closheens in Wine Sauce

Closheens, otherwise known as queen scallops, are to be found in great abundance in the deep bays off the West Coast of Ireland.

40 closheens
300 ml/½ pint dry white wine
salt and pepper
1 small onion, chopped
1 tablespoon chopped parsley
¼ teaspoon chopped thyme
1 clove of garlic, crushed
15 g/½ oz butter
1 tablespoon flour

Put the closheens in a saucepan with the wine, seasoning, onion, parsley, thyme and garlic. Bring to the boil and cook briskly until the shells open. Remove the closheens from the shells, discard the beards and black parts and rinse in fresh water. Strain the wine sauce into a clean pan and add the closheens. Adjust seasoning. Make a paste with the butter and flour. Bring the wine mixture just to the boil, add the butter and flour paste in small pieces and stir until the sauce thickens slightly. Simmer for 2 minutes. *Makes 4 servings.*

Fried Crubeens

It depends on the individual butcher whether the pickled trotters or crubeens need soaking before you cook them.

8 pig's trotters, pickled in brine
1 medium onion, chopped
1 medium carrot, sliced
1 bay leaf
generous pinch of pepper
1 tablespoon chopped parsley
1 egg, beaten
2 tablespoons dry brown breadcrumbs
fat to fry

Put the trotters, onion, carrot, bay leaf, pepper and parsley into a saucepan and cover with cold water. Bring to the boil, skim, cover and simmer for 2 hours, or until the trotters are tender. Remove the trotters and reserve the cooking stock for future use. Cut the trotters in half lengthways and remove the bones. Dip the meat in the beaten egg, coat with breadcrumbs and fry in hot fat until golden brown and crisp. *Makes 8 servings.*

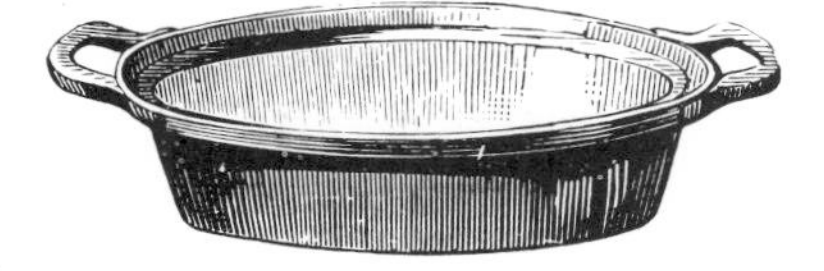

The Potato Crop

The recipes in this section all contain potatoes, the well-loved praties of Ireland.

Champ

Because so much butter is made in the Emerald Isle there is usually plenty of buttermilk for this dish and it is more frequently used than whole milk.

8 medium potatoes
1 medium onion
350 ml/12 fl oz milk or buttermilk
4 spring onions, trimmed
75 g/3 oz butter
salt and pepper

Cook the potatoes in lightly salted boiling water until just tender. Drain. Thinly slice the onion and cook in the milk for 5 minutes. Add to the cooked potatoes and mash well with the milk to give a creamy consistency. Finely chop the spring onions and beat into the potato mixture with the butter and seasoning to taste. *Makes 4 servings.*

Down Derry Dumplings

This recipe gives a useful method of combining the less presentable part of the pig (mainly the entrails), called chitterlings, with the inevitable potato.

1 kg/2 lb mashed potato
salt and pepper
100 g/4 oz cooked chitterling, chopped
50 g/2 oz onion, finely chopped
75 g/3 oz cheese, grated

Season the potato with salt and pepper and shape into balls the size of a dessert apple. Mix together the chitterling and onion, press a spoonful into the centre of each dumpling and reform the potato round it. Roll in grated cheese and stand on a greased baking tray. Bake in a hot oven (220°C, 425°F, Gas Mark 7) for 10–15 minutes, until the cheese is golden and melting. Serve immediately. *Makes 4–6 servings.*

A Hint from the Experts

The Irish people always boil potatoes in their jackets, which gives them a much better flavour. Take a small knife and cut about 1 cm/½ inch of peel right round the centre of the potato before boiling, so when they are cooked the potato skins can easily be removed with one pull at either end.

Irish Stew

Another dish which, like Haggis, is known round the world; and many slightly different recipes claim to be the authentic Irish Stew. This one comes from Cork and is wonderful filling fare.

1.5 kg/3 lb middle neck of lamb or mutton
1 kg/2 lb potatoes, sliced
2 large onions, sliced
salt and pepper
1 teaspoon dried mixed herbs
450 ml/$\frac{3}{4}$ pint stock or water

Cut the meat into even pieces, trimming off any excess fat. Arrange alternate layers of meat, potato and onion in a deep ovenproof casserole, seasoning each layer and sprinkling with herbs. Finish with a layer of potatoes. Pour over the stock. Cover and cook in a moderate oven (160°C, 325°F, Gas Mark 3) for 2 hours, or a little longer if the meat used is mutton. *Makes 6 servings.*

Pratie Cakes

These scone-like cakes are made for teatime guests and are served hot from the griddle, swimming in butter.

450 g/1 lb floury potatoes, freshly boiled
salt
about 25 g/1 oz flour

Drain and dry the potatoes. Push through a wire sieve on to a floured board, avoiding too much pressure so that the potatoes are very light. Season well with salt and scatter the flour over the top. Knead quickly but gently to make a light dough. Roll out to a thickness of 5 mm/$\frac{1}{4}$ inch and cut into 6-cm/$2\frac{1}{2}$-inch rounds with a biscuit cutter. Slide gently on to a fairly hot greased griddle and bake until rich brown on both sides. Butter thickly and serve straightaway. *Makes about 12.*

Right
The 'praties' of Ireland have become almost a way of life for the Irish, so often are they eaten, and in so many different forms. Here they are used in Dublin Coddle, a traditional regional dish. Ulster Baked Ham (foreground) is a succulent gammon joint with a delicious coating of butter, brown sugar and brandy.

Dublin Coddle

Here is a traditional dish, known since the Eighteenth Century. Originally leeks and oatmeal were used rather than the onions and potatoes which are more popular today.

8 rashers bacon, 5 mm/¼ inch thick
8 large pork sausages
1.25 litres/2¼ pints water
4 large onions, sliced
1 kg/2 lb potatoes, sliced
salt and pepper
chopped parsley or chives

Put the bacon rashers and sausages into a saucepan and cover with the water. Bring to the boil and cook for 5 minutes. Lift out the bacon and sausages and put into an ovenproof casserole, layering with the onion, potato, seasoning and a generous sprinkling of parsley or chives. Finish with a layer of potatoes and add sufficient cooking liquid almost to cover. Cover and cook in a moderate oven (160°C, 325°F, Gas Mark 3) for 1–1½ hours, or until cooked. Remove the lid halfway through to brown the top. Serve with soda bread and Guinness. *Makes 8 servings. Illustrated left.*

Colcannon

Vegetables are the mainstay of the Irish people and this tasty mixture is a great favourite, especially with children.

Equal quantities of cabbage, carrot, turnip and potato are finely sliced and all cooked together in one pot, then drained and mashed with a generous seasoning of brown table sauce and plenty of butter.

Ulster Baked Ham

The smoked hams of Ireland are famous throughout the world for their characteristic flavour and texture, mellow and fine-grained.

1.75 kg/4 lb joint of smoked
Ulster corner gammon
1 blade of mace
freshly ground pepper
50 g/2 oz butter
50 g/2 oz brown sugar
1 tablespoon brandy
150 ml/¼ pint ale or Guinness
watercress to garnish

Soak the bacon overnight in water. Drain and place in a saucepan with fresh water to cover. Add the mace and pepper to taste. Bring to the boil, cover and simmer for 1½ hours. Remove from the pan and cool slightly. Strip off the rind. Mix the butter, brown sugar and brandy together and spread over the fat surface. Stand the joint in an ovenproof dish and pour the ale around it. Bake in a moderately hot oven (190°C, 375°F, Gas Mark 5) for 30 minutes. Garnish with watercress and serve hot or cold, cut into slices. *Makes 8 servings. Illustrated left.*

Dodgers

100 g/4 oz Irish Cheddar cheese
25 g/1 oz plain flour
2 teaspoons baking powder
¼ teaspoon salt
1 tablespoon fine oatmeal
¼ teaspoon freshly ground black pepper
about 150 ml/¼ pint milk
½ teaspoon dried mixed herbs
fat or oil to fry

Cut the cheese into small dice. Sift the flour, baking powder and salt into a bowl and stir in the oatmeal and pepper. Add just sufficient milk to make a thick batter. Beat well. Stir in the cheese and herbs. Heat a little fat or oil in a large non-stick frying pan and add the batter, a tablespoon at a time, to make small fritters. Fry fairly quickly until golden brown on both sides, turning once. Drain well on absorbent paper. *Makes 8.*

Boxty Bread

In Ireland, the ubiquitous potato is used even in bread to eke out the precious supplies of flour. This is the favourite.

450 g/1 lb raw potatoes
450 g/1 lb mashed potato
350 g/12 oz plain flour
15 g/½ oz baking powder
1 teaspoon salt
100 g/4 oz butter, softened

Grate the raw potatoes on to a clean piece of muslin. Twist and squeeze slightly to remove excess moisture. In a basin mix thoroughly the grated potato, mashed potato, flour, baking powder, salt and butter. Turn the mixture out on to a floured surface and divide into four equal portions. Roll each into a round about 5 mm/¼ inch thick. Mark into farls (quarters). Place on a greased baking tray and bake in a moderate oven (180°C, 350°F, Gas Mark 4) for 40 minutes. Divide into quarters and serve very hot with plenty of butter. *Makes 16 farls.*

Boxty on the griddle,
Boxty in the pan,
The wee one in the middle,
It is for Mary Ann!
If you don't eat boxty,
You'll never get your man.

Boxty Pancakes

The most delicious pancakes can be made at the same time as baking a batch of Boxty bread.

Take half the quantities, adding ½ teaspoon of bicarbonate of soda with the flour, and more milk to give a dropping consistency. Cook spoonfuls of the mixture on a hot griddle for 3–4 minutes on each side until golden brown. Serve warm spread with butter and sprinkled with brown sugar.

Soda Bread

The use of yeast came very late in Ireland and even today soda bread may be preferred by many country housewives. To make a really good, delicate bread, it is essential to mix with buttermilk or, if not available, with sour milk.

450 g/1 lb plain flour
1 teaspoon salt
1 teaspoon bicarbonate of soda
25 g/1 oz butter
about 300 ml/½ pint buttermilk
or sour milk

Sift the flour, salt and bicarbonate of soda into a bowl. Rub in the butter and mix with the buttermilk to a soft dough. Shape quickly into a round 3.5–5 cm/1½–2 inches thick, place on a greased baking tray and mark with a knife into four or six wedges. Bake in a moderate oven (180°C, 350°F, Gas Mark 4) for 25–30 minutes.

If the buttermilk is not very rich, or if sour milk is used instead, a good pinch of cream of tartar should be added to the dry ingredients.

Note Only very light kneading is required and no proving as for a yeasted bread.

Irish Buttermilk Scones

450 g/1 lb plain flour
2 teaspoons bicarbonate of soda
2 teaspoons cream of tartar
1 teaspoon salt
75 g/3 oz lard
50 g/2 oz castor sugar
175 g/6 oz currants
about 450 ml/¾ pint buttermilk

Sift the flour, bicarbonate of soda, cream of tartar and salt into a bowl. Rub in the lard and stir in the sugar and currants. Add the buttermilk and mix with a knife, until the dough is smooth. Turn out on a floured surface and knead very lightly. Divide the dough in half and shape each portion into a round about 1 cm/½ inch thick. Put on greased baking trays, mark into portions and bake in a hot oven (220°C, 425°F, Gas Mark 7) for 8–10 minutes, or until well-risen and golden brown. *Makes* 2.

Lemon Whiskey Cake

A day's shooting is a popular pastime with country folk and usually provides meat for a good game stew. This cake is often served after the shoot for tea.

175 g/6 oz sultanas
thinly pared rind and juice of 1 large lemon
6 tablespoons whiskey
175 g/6 oz butter
175 g/6 oz castor sugar
3 eggs, separated
175 g/6 oz self-raising flour, sifted

Put the sultanas into a basin with the lemon rind and juice. Add the whiskey and leave overnight. The following day cream the butter and sugar until light and fluffy. Beat in the egg yolks, one at a time, with a spoonful of flour. Discard the lemon rind and add the sultanas and their liquid to the creamed mixture with the remaining flour. Whisk the egg whites until stiff and fold into the mixture. Turn into a greased and lined 20-cm/8-inch square cake tin. Bake in a moderate oven (160°C, 325°F, Gas Mark 3) for 1¼–1½ hours, until firm to the touch.

Guinness Cake

Guinness has been said to be to an Irishman as claret is to a Frenchman – more a way of life than merely a drink! Its full rich flavour adds something very special to this delicious moist cake.

225 g/8 oz butter, softened
225 g/8 oz soft brown sugar
4 eggs
275 g/10 oz plain flour
2 teaspoons ground mixed spice
225 g/8 oz seedless raisins
225 g/8 oz sultanas
100 g/4 oz glacé cherries, chopped
100 g/4 oz chopped mixed peel
100 g/4 oz walnuts, chopped
150 ml/¼ pint Guinness

Cream the butter and sugar together until light and fluffy. Gradually beat in the eggs. Sift the flour and spice and fold into the creamed mixture with the fruit, peel and nuts and 4 tablespoons of the Guinness. Mix well and turn into a greased and lined 18-cm/7-inch round cake tin. Bake in a moderate oven (160°C, 325°F, Gas Mark 3) for 1 hour. Reduce oven heat to cool (150°C, 300°F, Gas Mark 2) and bake for a further 1½ hours. Cool and turn out. Prick the base of the cake several times with a skewer and spoon over the rest of the Guinness. Store in an airtight tin for at least a week before cutting.

WALES

This country of soft rains and sweet voices bears the imprint of a Celtic heritage similar to that of Scotland. They resemble each other strongly in the sheer simplicity and economy of daily fare. But the fertile green valleys of which the Welsh Bards sing have no counterpart among the granite peaks of Scotland. The climate of Wales is milder, the soil more productive, and food more generous than in the spartan Scottish diet.

However, as in all Celtic countries, oatmeal is a favourite cereal. Oatcakes are as widely enjoyed as yeasted breads and baked in much the same way as in Scotland, on the flat iron plate which the Scottish cook calls a girdle, and the Welsh cook a bakestone or planc. In most households where they are frequently made, there's a crafell (wooden slice) to turn them, and an oatcake rack to dry them off before the fire. A favourite sandwich, especially in the northern counties of Wales, is made by placing an oatcake between two slices of bread.

Some of the old Welsh recipes have changed as oatmeal has been rejected in favour of flour. A thin pancake batter called 'bara bwff' was once made with a mixture of plain flour and oatmeal. Today, floury buttermilk scones are more popular. Even Trollins (or Trollies) were once made entirely of oatmeal, suet and currants, mixed with a little broth from the pot to form dumplings. Then they were cooked in the stew instead of potatoes when vegetables were scarce. Now they are almost always made with self-raising flour and served boiled as a sweet.

More changes are due to the development of the mining industry. As mining towns with their coal tips and slag heaps displace the rolling, verdant countryside, the sheep find fewer pastures to graze. The famous sweet mutton and lamb of Wales is less a feature of the local diet than it used to be. If seafood such as limpets, cockles, and the odd-tasting seaweed called laver are less often eaten, one glory remains: leeks still flourish in this, their accepted national home. A leek pasty in Wales is still considered food fit for a prince or a king.

Fertile green valleys, hills and mountains make this a landscape of gentle beauty.

Cockle Pie

Gathering cockles is a very old industry in Wales and these tiny shellfish are much prized for their delicate flavour. Women used to carefully scrape them up from the shore, wash them well in sea water and bring them home in baskets. Nowadays, if you buy shelled cockles from a fishmonger they may have been stored in brine. Wash them well and omit salt from the seasoning.

225 g/8 oz streaky bacon, derinded
225 g/8 oz shortcrust pastry
(made with 225 g/8 oz flour, etc.)
1 medium onion, finely chopped
1.75 litres/3 pints cooked cockles, shelled
salt and pepper
300 ml/½ pint cockle or fish stock
milk to brush

Chop the bacon. Roll out the pastry fairly thickly and use to line a deep 1.25-litre/2-pint pie dish, leaving sufficient pastry to cut out some narrow strips for the top of the pie. Layer the onion, bacon and cockles in the pastry case, seasoning each layer and finishing with a layer of cockles. Pour in the stock, moisten the pastry edges and cover with a lattice of pastry strips. Brush these with milk and bake in a moderately hot oven (200°C, 400°F, Gas Mark 6) for 30 minutes, or until golden brown. *Makes 6 servings.*

Limpet Pie This pie may be made with limpets instead of cockles and either of these shellfish may be used to replace the white fish in Whitby Pie (see page 62).

Trout with Bacon

Welsh lakes and rivers are well stocked with trout and trout farming is carried on in some districts. This dish is frequently served.

4 trout
8 thin rashers smoked streaky bacon, derinded
2 tablespoons chopped parsley
salt and pepper

Remove the heads from the trout and split, clean and fillet them. Line an ovenproof dish with half the bacon rashers. Cover with the trout and a sprinkling of parsley. Season well and top with the remaining bacon rashers. Bake in a moderately hot oven (200°C, 400°F, Gas Mark 6) for 15–20 minutes. *Makes 4 servings.*
Note Trout for grilling used to be cleaned then set in a large leek leaf, which made a container of the right shape and size.

Laver and Laverbread

Laver is an edible, smooth, fine seaweed which is gathered along the shores of South Wales where it can be bought from wooden tubs in some shops and markets. It is traditionally prepared using silver or wooden spoons.

It should be well washed to remove sand and grit, then boiled for 5–6 hours until tender. Drain and mix with sufficient oatmeal to make a thick paste – this is laverbread.

There are several ways to serve it: hot with melted butter, salt, pepper and a squeeze of lemon juice on buttered toast; shaped into cakes, coated with oatmeal and fried with the breakfast bacon then served on a thick slice of fried bread; mixed with a squeeze of Seville orange juice and served with roast Welsh lamb; cold with vinegar; added to mutton cawl (broth) or fish chowder.

Welsh Cheese Pudding

4–6 thick slices bread
butter to spread
225 g/8 oz Cheddar or other strong cheese, grated
salt and freshly ground pepper
½ teaspoon dry mustard
600 ml/1 pint milk
3 eggs

Remove the crusts from the bread and toast the slices on one side only. Butter the untoasted side and place two slices, butter side up, in the base of a buttered ovenproof dish. Cover with half the cheese and sprinkle with salt, pepper and mustard. Add the remaining slices of toast, the same way up, and top with the rest of the cheese and seasoning. Bring the milk to the boil and mix with the beaten eggs. Pour into the baking dish. Allow to stand for at least 30 minutes, then bake in a moderate oven (180°C, 350°F, Gas Mark 4) for 30 minutes, until well puffed up and golden brown. *Makes 3–4 servings. Illustrated overleaf.*

Leek Pasties

These pasties are traditionally made in the shape of a small, neatly trimmed leek. In the old days each one actually contained a whole leek, and when large leeks were used they made a substantial meal.

6 leeks, white parts only
1 teaspoon sugar
1 teaspoon lemon juice
450 g/1 lb shortcrust pastry
(made with 450 g/1 lb flour, etc.)
little cream
salt and pepper
milk or beaten egg to brush

Wash the trimmed leeks carefully under running water. Cut into 2.5-cm/1-inch lengths and place in a pan of salted water. Add the sugar and lemon juice and cook for 3–4 minutes. Drain well and cool. Roll out the pastry fairly thickly and cut into six oblongs, each 15 × 10 cm/6 × 4 inches. Arrange the leeks down the centre of each oblong, add a little cream and sprinkle with salt and pepper. Moisten the edges and raise the sides, pressing the pastry together to make a firm seal, and pinching in the ends. Brush with milk or beaten egg, place on a baking tray and bake in a moderately hot oven (200°C, 400°F, Gas Mark 6) for 20–25 minutes, until golden brown. *Makes 6. Illustrated overleaf.*

Glamorgan Sausages

This type of sausage is unique to Wales. It was originally made with Glamorgan cheese (no longer available) but is excellent made with strong Cheddar. Caerphilly is considered too mild.

100 g/4 oz fresh white breadcrumbs
100 g/4 oz cheese, grated
pinch of dried mixed herbs
pinch of dry mustard
1 teaspoon grated onion
salt and pepper
1 egg plus 1 egg white
dry breadcrumbs to coat
fat or oil to deep fry

Mix together the fresh breadcrumbs, cheese, herbs, mustard and onion and season well. Add the whole egg to the dry ingredients and mix thoroughly. Form into sausage shapes with floured hands. Whisk the egg white lightly until frothy. Dip the sausages into the egg white then coat in dry breadcrumbs, shaking off any surplus. Deep fry in hot fat or oil until crisp and golden brown. Drain on absorbent paper. *Makes about 10 small sausages. Illustrated overleaf.*

Welsh Rarebit

100 g/4 oz strong cheese, grated
25 g/1 oz butter
3 tablespoons milk
salt and pepper
pinch of dry mustard (optional)
4 slices hot buttered toast

Put the cheese, butter and milk into a saucepan and melt slowly over gentle heat, stirring. Add the salt, pepper and mustard to taste. Pour over the toast and brown under a hot grill. *Makes 4 servings.*
Note Beer is often used in place of milk.

Buck Rarebit A supper dish made in the same way as Welsh Rarebit, then topped with a poached egg.

Welsh Bacon Pie

175 g/6 oz streaky bacon, derinded
450 g/1 lb shortcrust pastry
(made with 450 g/1 lb flour, etc.)
65 g/2½ oz plain flour
900 ml/1½ pints milk
salt and pepper
3 eggs
2 tablespoons chopped parsley
1 teaspoon chopped chives
milk to brush

Dice the bacon. Roll out just over half the pastry and use to line a 1.25-litre/2-pint pie dish. Blend the flour with a little of the milk. Bring the rest of the milk to the boil, stir in the flour mixture and bring back to the boil, stirring constantly. Simmer for 2 minutes. Cool the sauce, season and beat in the eggs. Add the bacon and herbs, stirring until well mixed. Pour into the pastry-lined dish. Cover with the remaining pastry to make a lid, dampen the edges, seal well together and flute. Decorate with leaves made from the pastry trimmings. Brush with milk and bake in a moderately hot oven (200°C, 400°F, Gas Mark 6) for 50 minutes–1 hour. *Makes 8 servings. Illustrated overleaf.*

Overleaf
Welsh fare on a Welsh dresser; leeks and lamb are just two glorious survivors of this country's traditional cuisine. Shown here, from left: Leek Pasties, Breast of Welsh Lamb with Mint Sauce, Welsh Bacon Pie, Welsh Cheese Pudding and Glamorgan Sausages.

The Miser's Feast

The Miser responsible for this thrifty dish lived in Carmarthenshire and it has been popular ever since the early Nineteenth Century.

Thickly slice some potatoes and bring them to the boil in lightly salted water topped with thick onion rings and slices of gammon or bacon. Cover tightly and simmer until the meat is cooked and most of the water has been absorbed by the potatoes. Reserve the meat and serve the potatoes for one meal. The meat makes another meal to be eaten on the next day.

Breast of Welsh Lamb with Mint Sauce

2 (1.25-kg/2½-lb) breasts of lamb
25 g/1 oz flour
25 g/1 oz butter
2 small onions, sliced
900 ml/1½ pints stock
salt and pepper
450 g/1 lb shelled peas
pinch of sugar
Mint Sauce
1 tablespoon granulated sugar
2 teaspoons water
2 tablespoons finely chopped mint
2–3 tablespoons malt vinegar

Remove the skin and any excess fat from the breasts, cut the meat into neat pieces and toss in the flour. Melt the butter in a pan and cook the onions until soft. Add the meat and fry lightly until golden. Pour over the stock and season to taste. Bring to the boil, cover and simmer for 30 minutes. Add the peas and sugar and continue cooking until the peas are tender.

Meanwhile, make the mint sauce. Dissolve the sugar in the water and mix with the remaining ingredients. Allow to stand for 15 minutes. Hand separately to accompany the lamb and peas. *Makes 4–6 servings.* *Illustrated on preceding pages.*

Lleyn Rabbit Stew

225 g/8 oz streaky bacon, derinded
1 (1–1.5-kg/2¼–3-lb) rabbit, jointed
450 g/1 lb swede, diced
450 g/1 lb carrots, sliced
3 medium onions, sliced
salt and pepper
2 tablespoons chopped parsley
25 g/1 oz flour

Dice the bacon. Put the rabbit joints, bacon and vegetables into a large saucepan, season with salt and pepper and sprinkle with chopped parsley. Just cover with cold water. Bring to the boil, cover and simmer for about 1½ hours, until the rabbit is tender. Blend the flour to a smooth cream with a little cold water, stir well into the liquid gravy and bring to the boil, stirring gently all the time. Adjust seasoning. *Makes 6 servings.*

Welsh Salt Duck

The custom of salting the duck before cooking does not seem to be found anywhere else in the British Isles.

1 large plump duck
sea salt
2 onions, sliced
freshly ground pepper
Sauce
2 medium onions
40 g/1½ oz butter
25 g/1 oz flour
300 ml/½ pint single cream
salt and pepper

Remove the giblets and place the duck in a deep dish. Rub all over with plenty of sea salt. Cover with a clean cloth and leave in a cool place for 2–3 days, rubbing the duck with the salt twice daily. Place the giblets in a saucepan, cover with water and add half the sliced onion. Bring to the boil, cover and simmer for about 2 hours. Strain and reserve the stock.

Rinse the duck with running water and place in an ovenproof casserole. Surround with the remaining sliced onion and add 600 ml/1 pint of giblet stock. Season with pepper, cover with a lid and cook in a moderate oven (180°C, 350°F, Gas Mark 4) for about 2 hours, until the duck is tender.

Thirty minutes before the end of cooking time, make the sauce. Finely chop the onions, add 300 ml/½ pint stock from the casserole, bring to the boil, cover and simmer for about 20 minutes, until the onion is very soft. Melt the butter in a clean saucepan, stir in the flour and cook for 3 minutes without browning. Gradually add the onion and stock and bring to the boil, stirring constantly until the sauce thickens. Add the cream and continue stirring until the sauce is reheated almost to boiling point. Season to taste and hand separately with the duck. *Makes 4 servings.*

Note To serve cold allow the duck to cool in the stock, then pour over a mustard-flavoured French dressing.

Pikelets

These are sometimes known as crumpets or tea cakes. Many recipes exist, some of which include eggs and yeast. The following is an old recipe using the traditional buttermilk and bicarbonate of soda.

225 g/8 oz plain flour
40 g/1½ oz sugar
½ teaspoon salt
½ teaspoon bicarbonate of soda
buttermilk or sour milk to mix

Mix together the flour, sugar and salt and make a well in the centre. Dissolve the bicarbonate of soda in a little buttermilk and pour into the flour mixture. Beat well, adding sufficient buttermilk to make a thick batter. Grease a hot bakestone or heavy frying pan. Spoon on rounds of batter and cook over low heat until brown underneath. Turn and brown the other side. Butter and serve hot, with jam if liked. *Makes 15–18.* *Illustrated overleaf.*

Note Metal crumpet rings were originally used to preserve the true circular shape. A suitable alternative nowadays would be large plain greased metal biscuit cutters. Remove the ring to brown the other side.

Cree Cake

Cree is lard obtained by melting down pork belly fat. The lard makes excellent pastry and cakes.

450 g/1 lb self-raising flour
225 g/8 oz cree or lard, diced
225 g/8 oz sugar
milk to mix
sugar to sprinkle

Place the flour, cree and sugar in a mixing bowl. Add sufficient milk to make a soft dough. Turn out on a well-floured board and roll to a thickness of about 2.5 cm/1 inch. Place in a greased 20-cm/8-inch square cake tin, sprinkle lightly with sugar and bake in a moderately hot oven (180°C, 350°F, Gas Mark 4) for about 1 hour. A few currants are often added. *Illustrated overleaf.*

Bara

This word actually means sustenance in Welsh but it is generally taken to mean bread. There are many varieties, some baked in the oven and some on the bakestone, and on remote farms sufficient bread would be baked on one day to last for the whole week. On baking day a little of the bread dough was kept separate from the main batch and made into flat cakes to be cooked on the bakestone or floor of the oven. These were usually eaten hot for tea the same day with plenty of butter. Another custom was to set aside a little of the dough and knead into it some butter or lard, sugar and currants. This currant bread is the same everywhere in Wales but is known by almost as many names as there are places.

In some country districts bread is still made in a pot oven – a heavy iron pot with a lid, set on a trivet over an open fire out of doors.

Bara Planc

Here is a typical yeasted bread to be cooked on a hot bakestone (or planc), but it can easily be cooked in a heavy frying pan instead.

1 kg/2 lb plain flour
¼ teaspoon salt
50 g/2 oz fresh yeast
¼ teaspoon sugar
250 ml/8 fl oz warm milk
300 ml/½ pint warm water

Sift the flour and salt into a large warmed bowl. Cream the yeast with the sugar and a little warm water and leave for 10 minutes, until it becomes frothy. Make a well in the centre of the flour, pour in the yeast mixture and gradually add the milk and water to make a soft dough. Knead well. Cover and leave in a warm place until double in size. Divide the dough into portions and form each into a round flat loaf, patting it down firmly. Bake on a moderately hot bakestone for about 10–15 minutes, until brown on both sides. These are delicious split and buttered while hot. *Makes 6. Illustrated right.*

Right
A Welsh tea in front of a blazing log fire looks good enough to warm the heart and stomach of any fortunate passer-by. Bara Planc is cooking on the bakestone, while laid out on the table are (from top right) Cree Cake, Tinker's Cakes, Rice Grain Cake (in fingers) and Pikelets.

Planc Pastries

So called because they are baked on a planc or bakestone, these delicious pastry pies are made from rounds of sweet shortcrust pastry the size of a dinner plate. One round is covered with jam or fruit such as blackberries or gooseberries. A second round is placed on top, the edges sealed and then the pastry is baked on a moderately hot bakestone until golden brown on both sides. Turn carefully using a large fish slice. When cooked, split open and dot the hot fruit with butter, sprinkle with sugar and replace the top. If the pastry is filled with jam sprinkle the top with castor sugar. At harvest time these cakes would be made practically non-stop all day.

Tinker's Cake

450 g/1 lb cooking apples
450 g/1 lb self-raising flour
pinch of salt
225 g/8 oz butter
175 g/6 oz demerara sugar
milk to mix
sugar to sprinkle

Peel and core the apples and cut into small pieces or grate coarsely. Sift the flour and salt into a large mixing bowl. Rub in the butter until the mixture resembles fine breadcrumbs. Stir in the sugar and apple. Mix with sufficient milk to make a fairly stiff dough. Pat into a small greased roasting tin and bake in a moderately hot oven (200°C, 400°F, Gas Mark 6) for 40–50 minutes. Sprinkle with sugar and serve cut into squares.

This mixture can also be rolled out on a floured board and cut into rounds (as illustrated). Cook on a bakestone until golden brown on both sides, or on a greased baking tray in a moderately hot oven (200°C, 400°F, Gas Mark 6) for 30–40 minutes. *Makes 16 rounds. Illustrated on preceding pages.*

Spiced Potato Cakes

450 g/1 lb boiled potatoes
25 g/1 oz butter
25 g/1 oz sugar
pinch of salt
100 g/4 oz plain flour
1 teaspoon baking powder
½ teaspoon ground cinnamon
1 egg

Mash the potatoes while still warm. Add the butter and stir in the dry ingredients. Beat the egg and add to the mixture to make a smooth dough. Roll out on a floured surface to a thickness of 2.5 cm/1 inch, cut into 7.5-cm/3-inch rounds and place on greased baking trays. Bake in a hot oven (220°C, 425°F, Gas Mark 7) for 20 minutes. These cakes may also be cooked on a bakestone until nicely brown on both sides.

If a large cake is preferred the mixture should be placed in a greased 20-cm/8-inch cake tin. Bake in a hot oven as above for 20 minutes, then reduce the heat to moderate (180°C, 350°F, Gas Mark 4) for a further 45 minutes–1 hour. Serve hot or cold, split or sliced, with plenty of butter. *Makes about 10 small cakes or 1 large.*

Rice Grain Cake

In the old days this cake was baked in a Dutch oven in front of the fire. The unusual texture is best appreciated if the cake is eaten freshly baked, while still warm.

175 g/6 oz short-grain rice
450 g/1 lb plain flour
½ teaspoon freshly grated nutmeg
1 teaspoon baking powder
175 g/6 oz butter
100 g/4 oz castor sugar
4 large eggs, beaten
4 tablespoons milk

Boil the rice in salted water until soft and fluffy, but not mushy. Drain well. Sift the flour, nutmeg and baking powder into a bowl and rub in the butter until the mixture resembles fine breadcrumbs. Gently stir in the rice and sugar. Add the eggs and beat in the milk to make a soft batter. Pour into a well-greased 20 × 25-cm/8 × 10-inch roasting tin and bake in a moderately hot oven (200°C, 400°F, Gas Mark 6) for 1 hour, until firm to the touch. Serve cut into fingers. *Illustrated on preceding pages.*

Anglesey Dark Cake

275 g/10 oz plain flour
pinch of salt
pinch of ground mixed spice
pinch of ground ginger
100 g/4 oz mixed dried fruit
½ teaspoon bicarbonate of soda
300 ml/½ pint milk
100 g/4 oz lard
75 g/3 oz castor sugar
1 egg
1 tablespoon black treacle

Sift the flour, salt and spices into a bowl and stir in the dried fruit. Dissolve the bicarbonate of soda in the milk. Cream the lard and sugar until light and fluffy. Beat in the egg and stir in the flour mixture with the milk mixture and treacle. Beat until smooth and turn into a well-greased 20-cm/8-inch cake tin. Bake in a moderate oven (180°C, 350°F, Gas Mark 4) for 40–45 minutes, until firm to the touch.

Trollins

225 g/8 oz self-raising flour
pinch of salt
75 g/3 oz shredded suet
50 g/2 oz currants
pinch of freshly grated nutmeg
milk to mix
flour to coat
To Serve
demerara sugar
butter

Sift the flour and salt into a bowl. Stir in the suet, currants and nutmeg. Mix with milk to a stiff dough. Divide into eight pieces and mould each into a round. Dip in flour and flatten to a thickness of about 2 cm/¾ inch. Have ready a saucepan of boiling water and drop in the trollins, one at a time. Boil gently for 20 minutes. Drain well and serve very hot, generously sprinkled with demerara sugar and with a nut of butter melting on the top of each. *Makes 4 servings.*

Snowdon Pudding with Wine Sauce

Here is an exotic pudding; the name given to it in Welsh, Pwdin Eryi, actually means eagle's nest.

15 g/½ oz butter
75 g/3 oz seedless raisins
100 g/4 oz fresh white breadcrumbs
100 g/4 oz shredded suet
pinch of salt
75 g/3 oz soft brown sugar
finely grated rind of 1 lemon
3 eggs
75 g/3 oz lemon marmalade
Sauce
50 g/2 oz sugar
pared rind of ½ lemon
3 tablespoons water
1 teaspoon cornflour
15 g/½ oz butter
150 ml/¼ pint Madeira, sweet white wine or sherry

Grease a 1-litre/1¾-pint pudding basin with the butter then press on to the sides as many of the raisins as will adhere to the butter. Mix together the breadcrumbs, suet, salt, sugar and lemon rind. Beat the eggs and add to the dry ingredients with the marmalade and any remaining raisins. Spoon the mixture carefully into the prepared basin. Cover with greased greaseproof paper or foil with a pleat in the centre, and tie on securely. Place in a saucepan with boiling water to come halfway up the sides of the basin. Boil gently for about 1 hour, adding more boiling water if necessary.

Meanwhile, make the sauce. Simmer the sugar and lemon rind in the water for about 15 minutes then remove and discard the rind. Mix the cornflour and butter to a paste then stir briskly into the hot syrup. Add the wine, bring to the boil, stirring constantly, and simmer for about 10 minutes, until syrupy.

Turn the pudding out on to a warm serving plate and hand the sauce separately. For family meals the pudding is often served with a simple sweet white sauce. *Makes 6 servings.*

The North Country

It does not always rain in Manchester as rumour has it, but the climate of Northern England is both wetter and colder than in the South. There are traces of a 'kinship in the kitchen' where the ancient borders of Scotland and England meet at Hadrian's Wall. Near that border, several dishes made with oatmeal, like Tattie Hushie Soup, are still to be found.

This is not, however, one's first impression of the glories of North Country cooking. 'Wool and Mutton' was the great traditional toast, reminding us that sheep were the source of England's medieval wealth, and today traces of that golden age of pastoral plenty still survive. Sheep farming has always flourished on the blustery moors and fells, as indeed does dairy farming in the more sheltered valleys and plains. Wonderful cheeses – crumbly white Lancashire and Wensleydale, creamy Cheshire and the mellow orange Red Cheshire – bear witness to the good husbandry of Northern farmers. Cheese goes with everything, from fruit cake to apple tart. In a region where both east and west are bounded by the sea and the land is patchworked with rivers, fish is plentiful. Great fishing fleets still sail from Whitby, Fleetwood and Hull. Rich pies, hot pots and pastries abound, along with substantial cakes to warm the heart and keep out the cold.

But side by side with this great country cooking another tradition has risen up, beginning when the Industrial Revolution first laid a stark hand on the agrarian life of the North. Big cities have grown, swallowing up the countryside and bringing with them the din of the woollen mills and the smoke of the coal mines.

A new pattern of eating has emerged, suited to the needs of the miner and factory worker: Collier's Foot taken in a snap tin to be eaten down the pit; food like tripe and onions brought out from the tripe parlour for busy factory hands too tired to cook at home after a long day's shift.

The North has a rich heritage of hearty farmhouse cooking overlaid by the more recent influence of its manufacturing towns.

Cold winds in the North bring winter snow.

Soups

The bleak winters of Northern England make thick nourishing soups just as popular there as they are in Scotland. But the treasured soup recipes of Yorkshire and Lancashire include many made with pulses – lentils and peas – as well as the familiar mixture of oatmeal and potatoes.

Tattie Hushie

Just south of the Scottish border, recipes tend to have a Caledonian touch. This economical recipe using both potatoes and oatmeal is reminiscent of the kind of soup which is made superbly well in Scotland, as the title indicates.

1 large leek, sliced
675 g/1½ lb potatoes, diced
50 g/2 oz butter
25 g/1 oz medium oatmeal
1.15 litres/2 pints skimmed milk
salt and pepper
tomato ketchup (optional)

Rinse the leek well and simmer with the potato in boiling water to cover until tender. Drain and mash with the butter. Stir in the oatmeal, milk and seasoning then bring slowly to just below boiling point, stirring all the time. Serve with a little tomato ketchup stirred in, if wished. *Makes 6 servings.*

Cheshire Soup

A similar soup from Cheshire has grated cheese added just before serving.

450 g/1 lb potatoes, diced
2 medium leeks, chopped
2 medium carrots, diced
1.75 litres/3 pints chicken stock
50 g/2 oz medium oatmeal
salt and pepper
50 g/2 oz Cheshire cheese, grated

Simmer the vegetables in the stock for 15–20 minutes, until tender. Sprinkle in the oatmeal, and stir well. Season to taste and cook for a further 10 minutes. Stir in the cheese and serve immediately. *Makes 6 servings.*

Lentil Soup

225 g/8 oz lentils
2 large onions, chopped
2 large carrots, diced
1 small swede, diced
1 large leek, chopped
2 sticks celery, chopped
1 bacon knuckle
1.75 litres/3 pints water
salt and pepper
1 faggot of herbs

Cover the lentils with cold water and allow to soak overnight. Drain and place in a large saucepan with the prepared vegetables, bacon knuckle, water, seasoning and herbs. Bring to the boil and remove any scum. Simmer for about 1½ hours, until the lentils are soft. Taste and adjust the seasoning if necessary. The meat from the knuckle may be cut up and served with the soup to make a substantial meal or left until cold for sandwiches. *Makes 6–8 servings.*

Carlings

The 'carling' or black-skinned pea used to be served in many Yorkshire towns on Carling Sunday (Passion Sunday). The peas were soaked, boiled, well drained and fried in butter or with bacon, to a thick mush. Liberally seasoned, they are still enjoyed by hearty eaters who prefer them to the more familiar pease pudding.

Pace Eggs

Hard-boiled eggs are associated with many pre-Christian rites at the time of the great spring festival. Now, on Easter Sunday, 'Pace Eggers' or 'Jolly Boys' collect hard-boiled eggs, fruit and money from the audience for performing ancient morality plays. The eggs used to be decorated by boiling them with onion skins to colour the shells yellow. More elaborate decorative effects were achieved by wrapping the onion skins round the eggs together with ferns or flowers, covered with a layer of newspaper tied on with string. Often, after being admired, the eggs were rolled down a grassy hill to see whose shell lasted longest.

Fish

Fish and shellfish are good traditional fare on both the east and west coasts. There's said to be nothing better than Tweed salmon north or south of the Scottish border.

Baked Salmon or Salmon Trout with Cucumber

Nowadays salmon is a luxury but in bygone days it was plentiful and cheap. This recipe comes from Northam-on-Tweed, where Northumberland borders on Scotland. On February 14th, the opening of the salmon season, an ancient ceremony takes place there called 'The blessing of fishermen and nets'.

1 large cucumber, peeled and diced
salt
1.25–1.5-kg/2½–3-lb piece of salmon, or a salmon trout of the same weight
little melted butter
300 ml/½ pint dry white wine
pepper
300 ml/½ pint double cream

Sprinkle the cucumber with salt and allow to stand. Place the fish in a well-buttered ovenproof dish. Brush with melted butter, cover and cook in a moderate oven (160°C, 325°F, Gas Mark 3) for 20 minutes. Rinse and drain the cucumber and add to the fish with the wine and a sprinkling of pepper. Return to the oven for a further 20 minutes. Remove the upper skin from the fish, taking care not to break the flesh. Stir the cream carefully into the cucumber and wine mixture and baste the fish with some of this sauce. Adjust the seasoning if necessary. Heat through in the oven for about 5 minutes. *Makes 8 servings.*

Cumberland Shipped Herrings

8 herrings, with roes
50 g/2 oz fresh white breadcrumbs
1 small onion, chopped
1 teaspoon anchovy essence
65 g/2½ oz butter, melted
salt and pepper

Have the herrings cleaned and remove the backbones. Poach the roes for 2–3 minutes in boiling water then drain and chop. Add the breadcrumbs, onion, anchovy essence and 1 tablespoon of the melted butter. Season to taste. Divide the stuffing into eight portions, place each in a herring and pat it back into its original shape. Place close together in a buttered ovenproof dish and pour over the remaining butter. Bake in a moderately hot oven (190°C, 375°F, Gas Mark 5) for 20 minutes. *Makes 8 servings.*

Whitby Pie

This dish is usually served on Good Friday.

225 g/8 oz plain flour
pinch of salt
100 g/4 oz lard
butter for pie dish
milk to brush
Filling
450 g/1 lb cod fillet
100 g/4 oz ham, thinly sliced
2 eggs, hard-boiled and sliced
salt and freshly ground pepper

Sift the flour and salt into a bowl. Rub in the lard with the fingertips until the mixture resembles fine breadcrumbs. Add just sufficient cold water to mix to a stiff dough. Allow to rest in a cool place while preparing the filling.

Place the fish in a saucepan, cover with cold water and bring to the boil. Simmer for 10–15 minutes, until the fish is cooked. Drain and reserve the stock. Remove any skin and bones from the fish, flake it and place in a buttered 1-litre/1¾-pint pie dish. Cover with the ham and a layer of sliced hard-boiled egg. Season with salt and pepper and pour over 150 ml/¼ pint of the fish stock. Roll out the pastry to cover the pie and decorate with a fish cut out from the trimmings. Brush with milk and bake in a moderately hot oven (200°C, 400°F, Gas Mark 6) for 20–25 minutes. *Makes 4–6 servings. Illustrated right.*

Morecambe Bay Potted Shrimps

Since the Eighteenth Century surplus shrimps have been potted and sold at many coastal resorts. Those from Morecambe are regarded as the most delicately flavoured.

1.25 litres/2 pints freshly boiled shrimps, shelled
1 teaspoon ground mace
¼ teaspoon ground ginger
salt
pinch of cayenne pepper
175 g/6 oz butter

Mix the shrimps with the mace and ginger and season to taste with salt and cayenne pepper. Melt three-quarters of the butter but do not let it boil. Add the seasoned shellfish and stir over a low heat until the shrimps have absorbed the butter. Remove from the heat and press into small pots. Melt the remaining butter and pour over the top of the shrimps while they are still warm. Store in the refrigerator and serve with fingers of hot toast. *Makes 4 servings. Illustrated right.*

Lobster Pancakes

Until a few years ago the fishermen's wives, wearing their traditional bonnets, still sold lobsters, crabs and other fish in Stockton Market. Nowadays the lobsters go straight to London.

12 cooked pancakes
Sauce
450 ml/¾ pint milk
1 small onion, chopped
1 bay leaf
3 peppercorns
50 g/2 oz butter
25 g/1 oz flour
salt and pepper
1 lobster, boiled
generous pinch of paprika pepper
50 g/2 oz hard cheese, grated

Place the milk, onion, bay leaf and peppercorns in a saucepan. Bring gently to the boil, remove from the heat, cover and allow to cool. Strain. Melt half the butter in a clean saucepan, stir in the flour and cook for 2 minutes. Gradually add the strained milk and bring to the boil, stirring constantly, until the sauce is smooth and thickened. Simmer for 3 minutes. Season to taste, remove from the heat and cover with a circle of damp greaseproof paper.

Take the flesh from the lobster and chop it. Include the coral if this is available. Melt the remaining butter in a frying pan, add the chopped lobster meat and coral and the paprika pepper. Stir until really hot then add about a quarter of the sauce. Fill the pancakes with this mixture, roll them up and place close together in a shallow ovenproof dish. Pour over the remaining sauce and sprinkle with the cheese. Heat through in a moderately hot oven (190°C, 375°F, Gas Mark 5) for 20 minutes. *Makes 6 servings.*

Right
The North Country still lands great catches of fish, which are sent to outlets all over the country. The fish used in Whitby Pie (centre) varies according to the catch, but some would say nothing can compare with the flavour of freshly potted shrimps (foreground), and those from Morecambe Bay are highly prized.

Meat, Poultry and Game

Hot pots and pies are solid favourites in this region, and the pastry is often made with dripping instead of butter. Pot pies are the equivalent of the suet pastry puddings of the South.

Lancashire Hot Pot

This stew was always made and served in a deep brown earthenware pot, sold especially for the purpose, and accompanied by pickled red cabbage.

4 mutton chops or large lamb chops
3 sheeps' kidneys
450 g/1 lb onions, sliced
1 kg/2 lb potatoes, sliced
salt and pepper
450 ml/¾ pint hot beef stock or water
50 g/2 oz butter or dripping

Trim the chops if necessary. Skin, halve, core and slice the kidneys. Place the chops in an ovenproof dish. Add layers of kidney, onion and potato, seasoning each layer and ending with a layer of potatoes. Pour over the hot stock and dot the surface with the butter or dripping. Cover and cook in a moderate oven (160°C, 325°F, Gas Mark 3) for 3 hours. Remove the lid 30 minutes before serving to brown the top. *Makes 4 servings.*

Cumberland Hot Pot This contains stewing beef in place of some of the chops.

Lakeland Hot Pot This variation includes slices of black pudding.

Bolton Hot Pot This dish contains mushrooms and oysters as well as the meat.

Lancashire Foot

This was a thick oval pasty which fitted into a miner's snap tin. The name indicated its shape. A thick oval of pastry was cut in two along its length. Each piece was rolled from the centre to the far end thus enlarging it to form the sole, leaving the thicker heel near the cook. This heel formed the base and was covered with a filling of meat, potato, onion and seasoning, then the sole was folded over the top and sealed down all round. The remaining pastry was used to make a second pasty so the miner got a pair of them in his tin for lunch.

Collier's Foot *The pastry for this was often made from bacon fat and the filling consisted of onion, cheese and bacon with a little mustard.*

Boiled Beef in Beer

1.75 kg/4 lb stewing steak
1 kg/2 lb onions, sliced
1 faggot of herbs
(parsley, thyme, marjoram)
2 cloves
12 peppercorns
4 tablespoons wine vinegar
100 g/4 oz black treacle
1.15 litres/2 pints light ale
salt and pepper

Trim and cut the steak into cubes. Place in a dish and cover with sliced onions and the herbs. Combine the cloves, peppercorns, vinegar and treacle and mix well. Pour over the onions and meat, cover and leave to stand in a cool place overnight.

The following day put the contents of the dish into a large saucepan with the ale. Bring to the boil and simmer for 3 hours. Taste and season if necessary. Serve with boiled potatoes and red or green cabbage. *Makes 12 servings.*

Potted Beef

Potted meat and fish were often features of the Northern high tea. Potted beef is made from the shin (called hough in Scotland where it is known as Potted Hough).

450 g/1 lb shin of beef
1 small onion stuck with 4 cloves
1 blade of mace
450 ml/¾ pint water
1½ teaspoons salt
pepper

Cut the beef into small pieces. Put in a flameproof casserole with the onion, mace and water and bring slowly to the boil. Remove any scum carefully with a slotted spoon and season the mixture with the salt and pepper to taste. Cover with a close-fitting lid and cook in a cool oven (150°C, 300°F, Gas Mark 2) for 3 hours.

Remove the onion and mace and discard. Chop the meat finely or shred it with two forks. Place in a basin and strain over sufficient stock to cover. When cold the meat should be set in a delicious jelly. Turn out to serve. *Makes 4 servings.*

Note For a stronger flavour and a more firmly set jelly, a pig's trotter may be cooked with the meat.

Lancashire Tripe and Onions

In the industrial towns of the North West, tripe parlours were once as common as fish and chip shops. This dish was usually served with mashed potatoes.

1 kg/2 lb dressed tripe
350 g/12 oz onions, sliced
900 ml/1½ pints milk
50 g/2 oz butter
25 g/1 oz flour
salt and pepper
pinch of freshly grated nutmeg

Wash the tripe and cut into 5-cm/2-inch squares. Cover with water and bring to the boil. Drain off and discard the water. Add the sliced onion to the tripe with the milk and simmer for 1½ hours, until tender. Melt the butter in a clean pan, stir in the flour and cook for 3 minutes. Gradually add the milk from the tripe to make a sauce. Bring to the boil, stirring constantly, and season to taste with salt, pepper and nutmeg. Add the tripe and onions and heat thoroughly. *Makes 6 servings.*

Boiled Pork and Pease Pudding

1 kg/2 lb yellow split peas
1–1.5 kg/2–3 lb pickled pork
(shoulder, hand or belly)
6 large onions, halved
6 large carrots, halved
4 sticks celery, chopped
1 small swede, sliced
6 peppercorns
25 g/1 oz butter
1–2 egg yolks (optional)
salt and pepper

Cover the split peas with cold water and leave to soak overnight. Simmer the meat for 10 minutes in about 1.75 litres/3 pints water. Skim the surface well. Add the vegetables and peppercorns and continue to simmer for 2–3 hours, according to the weight of the pork. Drain the soaked peas and tie in a muslin cloth or bag, allowing space for the peas to expand during cooking. Add to the pan for the last 1½ hours cooking time. When cooked turn the peas into a basin, stir in the butter and egg yolks and season well. Place in a saucepan, add boiling water to come halfway up the sides, cover and steam for 20 minutes.

Serve the pork and vegetables with the pease pudding, separately boiled cabbage and English mustard. *Makes 10–12 servings.*

Cumberland Sweet Pie

This interesting recipe still made at Christmas combines meat with plentiful spices and seasoning as well as sugar and dried fruit. As in the original mincemeat of the South, these ingredients helped to preserve the meat.

225 g/8 oz fat mutton chops
175 g/6 oz currants
175 g/6 oz seedless raisins
175 g/6 oz sultanas
50 g/2 oz candied lemon peel, chopped
100 g/4 oz soft brown sugar
ground mace, cinnamon and nutmeg
salt and pepper
juice of 1 lemon
150 ml/¼ pint rum
225 g/8 oz shortcrust pastry
(made with 225 g/8 oz flour, etc.)
milk to brush

Bone the chops, cut the meat into small pieces and put into the base of a greased 1-litre/1½-pint pie dish. Mix the dried fruits, peel and sugar with a generous pinch of each of the spices, and seasoning to taste. Spread over the meat. Pour in the lemon juice and rum. Roll out the pastry to cover the pie, using any trimmings to make holly leaves to decorate the top. Make a steam vent in the centre and brush with milk. Bake in a moderately hot oven (200°C, 400°F, Gas Mark 6) for 35–40 minutes. *Makes 6–8 servings. Illustrated overleaf.*

Buttered Grouse

The grouse of the Yorkshire moors is reputed to be one of the fullest flavoured and most delicious of game birds. This recipe is for a cold dish to serve on special occasions.

1 brace of grouse, plucked, cleaned
and trussed
50 g/2 oz dripping, softened
175 g/6 oz butter
½ teaspoon ground mace
salt and pepper
generous pinch of cayenne pepper

Spread the grouse with softened dripping and place in a roasting tin. Roast in a moderately hot oven (200°C, 400°F, Gas Mark 6) for 15–20 minutes, until tender, basting two or three times. Remove any string from the birds, joint them and place in a shallow serving dish. Melt the butter and add to it a tablespoon of the dripping in which the birds were cooked. Stir in the mace and seasonings. Pour over the grouse and leave until quite cold. *Makes 4 servings.*

Durham Pot Pie

175 g/6 oz plain flour
75 g/3 oz shredded suet
pinch of salt
Filling
4 young rabbit portions
1 onion, quartered
1 leek, sliced
2 tablespoons chopped parsley
salt and pepper
150 ml/¼ pint water

Mix the flour, suet and a pinch of salt to a fairly stiff paste with a little water. Cut off a small piece and roll into a band 5 cm/2 inches deep, to fit round the inside top of a 1-litre/1½-pint pudding basin. Add the rabbit portions, onion, leek, chopped parsley and seasoning to taste. Pour in the water. Roll out the remaining pastry to form a lid, moistening the edges and sealing well to the collar. Cover with a floured cloth or greased foil. Stand the pot pie in a saucepan containing boiling water to come about halfway up the sides. Cover and boil for 3–3½ hours, adding more boiling water when necessary. *Makes 4 servings. Illustrated right.*

Variation Use 575 g/1¼ lb stewing steak and 100 g/4 oz ox kidney, cubed and tossed in seasoned flour, with 1 large chopped onion, and 150 ml/¼ pint water.

Yorkshire Roast Goose

Long before the turkey was introduced in the Sixteenth Century, goose was the traditional festive bird of Britain. The goose also provided down and feathers for pillows, cushions and mattresses, and the goose grease was spread on bread, used for frying, as a poultice, rubbed on chests for coughs and colds, and on chapped hands.

One way of making the goose go further was to fill its cavity not only with sage and onion stuffing, but with a whole or jointed rabbit as well. These inside pieces were given to the children as, being less rich, they were more easily digested, although still imbued with the flavour of the goose and its stuffing. Sometimes the rabbit was roasted in the same tin under the rack holding the goose.

Right
After the shoot. Succulent young rabbit portions go to make up Durham Pot Pie (right), and, to satisfy the sportsman's hearty appetite, Cumberland Sweet Pie (left) is a luscious combination of meat, spices and fruits.

Poor Man's Goose

Put layers of sliced potato, onion and ox liver into a pie dish or heavy pan. Season each layer with salt, pepper and a little dried sage. Top with a layer of sliced potato, add enough water to come halfway up, cover and cook in a moderate oven (160°C, 325°F, Gas Mark 3) for 2 hours, or over a gentle heat until all is tender.

Cousin Jim This requires the same ingredients as Poor Man's Goose but a few slices of bacon are added with the liver, and the sage is omitted.

Pans and Pots

The 'Pans' seem to be a feature of the cooking of the North East whereas, with the exception of Durham Pot Pie, the 'Pots' are to be found west of the Pennines.

Panackelty

Put diced cold beef or bacon into a frying pan with sliced raw onions. Add gravy and seasoning, cover with sliced raw potatoes and cook until tender.

Panjotheram

Slice potatoes into a deep pie dish until about two-thirds full. Put a mutton chop on top for each person. Season well and add boiling water to come halfway up the dish. Cover with a lid, plate or foil and cook in a moderate oven (160°C, 325°F, Gas Mark 3) for about 2 hours.

Pan Haggarty

Cut 450 g/1 lb potatoes and 225 g/8 oz onions into very thin slices. Heat a little dripping in the base of a frying pan. Put in a layer of potatoes. Cover with the onion, about 100 g/4 oz grated cheese and the rest of the potato slices, seasoning each layer with salt and pepper. Fry over a very gentle heat until almost cooked through. Invert on to a plate and slide back into the pan to brown the other side or, if preferred, brown the top under a hot grill. *Makes 4 servings.*

Lancashire Cheese Savoury

This recipe is a good standby to use up crumbly Lancashire cheese.

4 rashers streaky bacon
1 small onion, finely chopped
225 g/8 oz Lancashire cheese, finely crumbled
4 slices bread

Remove the rind from the bacon and chop finely. Sauté lightly with the onion. Mix with the crumbled cheese to make a thick paste. Toast the slices of bread on one side only. Spread the other sides with the mixture and grill slowly until puffed and golden. *Makes 4 servings.*

Yorkshire Pudding

This Yorkshire speciality is, perhaps, the world's most famous pudding and is served with roast beef in many countries. In the North of England it may be served with other roast meats as well. Originally it was cooked under the meat rack so that it became permeated with the juices that dripped from the meat. Though it used to be eaten with gravy before the meat, to take the edge off the appetite, it now accompanies it.

The pudding may also be eaten as a sweet, and served with jam or golden syrup. In parts of the North it is still cooked in meat dripping or lard even when intended to be eaten as a sweet.

100 g/4 oz plain flour
½ teaspoon salt
1–2 eggs
300 ml/½ pint milk
2 tablespoons water
25 g/1 oz dripping

Put the flour and salt into a bowl. Add the egg and mix into the flour. Gradually add the milk and water, beating well with each addition to make sure there are no lumps. The batter should be the consistency of thin cream. Let it stand for at least 30 minutes before use.

Heat the oven to hot (220°C, 425°F, Gas Mark 7). Put a little dripping in the base of a baking tin and heat in the oven until smoking hot. Pour the batter into the tin and bake for 15–25 minutes, or until well risen and golden brown. *Makes 4 servings.*

Herb Pudding Chopped boiled onions and sage are added to the batter.

Toad-in-the-Hole The batter is poured over partly cooked sausages.

Manx Mushroom Roll

The quality of Manx kippers is famous but the following recipe which is popular in the Isle of Man seems never to have been exported.

To make it you require about 350 g/12 oz suet pastry (made with 350 g/12 oz flour, etc.) rolled out into a large oblong. Cover the surface closely with 450 g/1 lb small mushroom caps. Fill the caps with softened butter and sprinkle with salt and pepper. Roll up carefully from the long edge, Swiss roll fashion, dampen and seal the edges. Wrap in greased greaseproof paper or foil to keep the shape, over-wrap in a floured pudding cloth tied at each end and steam gently for 2 hours. *Makes 6 servings.*

Rowan and Crab Apple Jelly

This lovely red jelly with a sharpish flavour and unusual smoky tang is delicious served with lamb or game as a change from redcurrant jelly.

rowan berries
crab apples, roughly chopped
450 g/1 lb preserving sugar for each 600 ml/1 pint juice

Put the fruit into a preserving pan or large saucepan, cover with water and simmer for 10–15 minutes, until a soft pulp. Strain overnight through a jelly bag or several layers of muslin. Measure the juice and return to the pan with 450 g/1 lb sugar to each 600 ml/1 pint of juice. Heat gently to dissolve the sugar then bring to the boil and cook rapidly for about 5–10 minutes, until a little jelly sets on a cold saucer. Pot while hot in warmed jars.

Avoid overcooking the berries as they develop a bitter flavour after about 15 minutes.

Sweets

The special character of cakes in the North Country is their solidity and frequent richness. Butter and dripping are used with a lavish hand.

Thor Cake

This ginger cake or parkin is nowadays served round the bonfire on Guy Fawkes Night with mugs of elderberry wine. The ceremony in fact pre-dates Guy Fawkes, and the cake is named in honour of the Norse God, Thor.

450 g/1 lb medium oatmeal
pinch of salt
15 g/½ oz ground ginger
pinch of ground mace
pinch of freshly grated nutmeg
100 g/4 oz chopped mixed peel
225 g/8 oz butter
225 g/8 oz soft brown sugar
100 g/4 oz black treacle
1 egg, beaten

Combine the oatmeal, salt, spices and peel in a large bowl. Warm the butter, sugar and treacle until the butter melts. Add to the flour mixture with the beaten egg and beat together until smooth. Pour into a greased and lined 20-cm/8-inch square cake tin. Bake in a moderate oven (160°C, 325°F, Gas Mark 3) for 45 minutes–1 hour, until firm to the touch. Keep for at least a week.

Yorkshire Apple Cake

The local cheese, Wensleydale, is eaten in beautiful, crumbly wedges with any kind of sweet apple cake or pie. There is a saying in the North of England that 'an apple pie without some cheese is like a kiss without a squeeze'. Here, the cheese is inside.

350 g/12 oz shortcrust pastry
(made with 350 g/12 oz flour, etc.)
4 cooking apples, peeled, cored and sliced
50 g/2 oz Wensleydale cheese, grated
50–75 g/2–3 oz castor sugar

Roll out half the pastry to line a Swiss roll tin. Layer the sliced apples, cheese and sugar over the pastry. Roll out the remaining pastry to make a lid and pinch the edges together with a fork to seal. Brush the top with water and sprinkle with sugar. Cook in a moderately hot oven (200°C, 400°F, Gas Mark 6) for 25 minutes, then cover with foil and reduce to 180°C, 350°F, Gas Mark 4 for 30–40 minutes. Serve cut in slices. *Makes about 16.* *Illustrated overleaf.*

Tea interval. In Yorkshire, cricket is a serious business, but then so is the cricket tea. This is sustaining fare. From left: Yorkshire Apple Cake with cheese, Yorkshire Curd Tarts, Eccles Cakes, Yorkshire Tea Cake and Bakewell Tart.

Yorkshire Curd Tarts

These tarts taste especially good eaten hot.

225 g/8 oz fresh curds or curd cheese (see note)
50 g/2 oz castor sugar
50 g/2 oz currants
3 eggs, beaten
1 tablespoon rum
75 g/3 oz butter, melted
225 g/8 oz shortcrust pastry (made with 225 g/8 oz flour, etc.)
freshly grated nutmeg

Place the curds in a basin and break up with a fork. Add the sugar, currants, beaten eggs, rum and melted butter and mix well. Roll out the pastry and use to line a 20-cm/8-inch flan tin or 24 individual bun tins. Pour in the filling mixture and sprinkle with nutmeg. Bake in a moderate oven (180°C, 350°F, Gas Mark 4) for about 25–30 minutes, until the filling is firm. *Makes 1 large or 24 small tarts. Illustrated on preceding pages.*
Note To make fresh curds, add 1 tablespoon lemon juice to 600 ml/1 pint of fairly hot (not boiling) milk. Leave until the curds form, then strain off the whey. 600 ml/1 pint milk gives 75–100 g/3–4 oz curds.

Eccles Cakes

Other towns have their own version of these rich little pastry cakes. For instance, Coventry Godcakes are very similar but have three slashes on top to represent the Trinity.

450 g/1 lb prepared puff pastry
100 g/4 oz currants
25 g/1 oz butter, softened
25 g/1 oz soft brown sugar
25 g/1 oz chopped mixed peel
1 egg white
castor sugar to sprinkle

Roll out the pastry to a thickness of 5 mm/¼ inch and cut into 10-cm/4-inch rounds. Mix the currants with the butter, sugar and peel and place a heaped teaspoon on each round. Moisten the edges with water, gather together in the centre and pinch firmly to seal. Turn the rounds over and roll out gently until the fruit begins to show through the pastry. Place on a dampened baking tray, score across the surface to make a chequered pattern, brush with lightly beaten egg white and sprinkle with castor sugar. Bake in a hot oven (220°C, 425°F, Gas Mark 7) for 20 minutes, or until puffed and golden brown. *Makes about 15. Illustrated on preceding pages.*

Yorkshire Tea Cakes

450 g/1 lb plain flour
¼ teaspoon salt
50 g/2 oz lard
50 g/2 oz butter
50 g/2 oz sugar
25 g/1 oz fresh yeast
300 ml/½ pint milk
1 egg, well beaten
milk to brush

Sift the flour and salt into a large bowl. Rub in the lard and butter lightly. Reserve 1 teaspoon sugar and add the rest to the flour mixture. Make a well in the centre.

Cream the yeast with the reserved sugar. Warm the milk to blood heat and mix with the egg. Add this to the yeast. Mix well and pour into the centre of the dry ingredients. Sprinkle over a little flour from the sides and leave in a warm place for 30 minutes, until frothy. Beat in all the flour to make a slack dough. Turn out on a floured board and knead well. Return to the bowl, cover and leave to rise for about 1 hour, or until double in size. Divide into two portions, knead each lightly and shape into a round. Place on greased baking trays, cover and leave to prove in a warm place for 20 minutes. Brush with warm milk and bake in a hot oven (220°C, 425°F, Gas Mark 7) for 10 minutes, then reduce heat to moderate (180°C, 350°F, Gas Mark 4) for a further 10 minutes. Cool, split and spread with butter to serve, toasted if preferred. *Makes 2. Illustrated on preceding pages.*

Bakewell Pudding or Tart

This famous pudding which is really a pastry tart, was invented by the cook at the Rutland Arms Hotel in Bakewell, who misunderstood her instructions and put the wrong filling into the pastry case. The result was so delicious that it became extremely popular, and the Olde Pudding Shop in Bakewell now claims to sell six thousand tarts every market day.

225 g/8 oz rich shortcrust pastry (made with 225 g/8 oz flour, 100 g/4 oz butter, 25 g/1 oz castor sugar, 1 egg yolk and 1–2 tablespoons water)
2 tablespoons raspberry jam
100 g/4 oz butter, melted
100 g/4 oz castor sugar
4 eggs, beaten
100 g/4 oz ground almonds

Roll out the pastry and use to line a 20-cm/8-inch flan ring or a 15-cm/6-inch ovenproof oval dish about 5 cm/2 inches deep.

Spread the jam over the pastry. Beat the butter and sugar together until light and fluffy. Gradually add the beaten eggs and ground almonds. Pour into the pastry case and bake in a moderately hot oven (200°C, 400°F, Gas Mark 6) for about 30–40 minutes, until the filling is set. *Makes 6 servings.* *Illustrated on preceding pages.*

Variation A more economical version can be made by substituting 50 g/2 oz plain flour for 50 g/2 oz ground almonds, in which case add a few drops of almond essence with the beaten egg.

Singing Hinny

Hinnies are so called because they sizzle and sing while they cook on the griddle. Hinny is a term of affection given to children in the North East where everyone is fond of this fruity teatime treat.

225 g/8 oz plain flour
½ teaspoon salt
50 g/2 oz butter
50 g/2 oz lard
50 g/2 oz sugar
50 g/2 oz currants
1 teaspoon baking powder
milk and/or sour cream to mix

Sift the flour and salt into a bowl. Rub in the butter and lard until the mixture resembles fine breadcrumbs. Stir in the remaining dry ingredients and mix to a stiff dough with milk and/or sour cream. Shape into a ball and roll out to a round about 1 cm/½ inch thick. Heat and grease the griddle. Place the hinny in the centre and prick the top with a fork. Cook for about 5 minutes on each side until brown.

Wakes Cake Made by the rubbed-in method, as for Singing Hinny, this rather more exciting version includes caraway seeds and chopped lemon peel as well as currants, and is made into a biscuit paste with a lightly beaten egg instead of milk or sour cream. The paste is rolled out and cut into small rounds, sprinkled with sugar and then baked in a moderately hot oven like biscuits.

Scarborough Pudding

A lovely summer pudding made with early plums or later in the season with damsons.

75 g/3 oz tapioca
butter for pie dish
75 g/3 oz sugar
600 ml/1 pint water
225 g/8 oz red plums or damsons

Wash and drain the tapioca. Place in a buttered pie dish with the sugar and water. Stir well. Remove the stones from the fruit and, if large, halve fruit. Add to the other ingredients and bake in a moderate oven (160°C, 325°F, Gas Mark 3) for 1 hour. Serve warm with cream. *Makes 4 servings.*

Cumberland Rum Butter

Traditionally served with Christmas pudding and mince pies, this hard sauce can also be used for filling cakes or to accompany other steamed puddings. It may be pressed into small pots or jars and stored in the refrigerator for several weeks.

225 g/8 oz unsalted butter
350 g/12 oz soft brown sugar
175 ml/6 fl oz rum
pinch of freshly grated nutmeg
pinch of ground cinnamon

Cream the butter and sugar until soft and fluffy. Blend in the rum a little at a time and flavour with the spices. *Makes 8 servings.*

Doncaster Butterscotch

450 g/1 lb brown sugar
300 ml/½ pint milk
175 g/6 oz butter
pinch of cream of tartar

Dissolve the sugar in the milk over a low heat then add the butter and cream of tartar and stir well. Bring to a full rolling boil and boil steadily until a little of the mixture hardens when tested in cold water. Pour in a thin layer into greased tins and allow to set. Break up when cold and store in an airtight tin. *Makes about 575 g/1¼ lb.*

The Midland Shires

At the very heart of England lie those famous counties renowned for 'hunting, shooting and fishing', the glorious Shires. Here the climate is more stable, drier and warmer than in the extreme North; but here too rural life has been eroded by industry. Fortunately much remains of the rolling acres of pastureland, the legendary forest glades; of copse, stream and clearing which once echoed to the twang of the bow. Food is rich, varied and plentiful.

Hunting is still in the blood of the men of the Shires. The pursuit of furred and feathered game is not only a sport, it is a serious business of providing food for the pot. So is coarse fishing. Because of the region's rich grazing, the Midlands have always excelled in dairy products and beef. The recipes in this section reflect a well-rounded agricultural economy, and are particularly interesting. There is a shift in emphasis from lamb and mutton, favoured in the North and West of England, to beef and especially dishes made with beef suet.

Market towns have been a feature of country life since the Middle Ages. There are many old towns in the Midlands whose names have been bestowed on local delicacies, such as Banbury Cakes and Gloucester Tarts. These were originally made for folk to eat while they strolled round the market, but the recipes have so well stood the test of time that they are now made daily by bakers as a matter of course.

If the Midlands have any special claim to an aspect of cooking in which they reign supreme, it must be in the creation of those marvellous raised pies made with hot water crust pastry and delicious fillings of pork and ham or delicate veal. It is said you have not savoured life to the full until you have tasted a Melton Mowbray pie!

The impact of industrial progress on nature is not always as beautiful as this; the Iron Bridge straddles the River Severn, while the fishermen below contentedly pass the day.

Izaak Walton's Pike Recipe

The most famous of all writers on the subject of freshwater fishing described this recipe as being 'too good for any but anglers or very honest men'. Perhaps he had it in mind that anglers do not always stick to the truth when describing the size of the fish they catch!

1 medium pike (about 2.75 kg/6 lb)
100 g/4 oz smoked or pickled oysters
4 anchovy fillets
2 sprigs of thyme
2 sprigs of marjoram
2 sprigs of winter savory
450 g/1 lb butter
salt and pepper
pinch of ground mace
½ bottle claret or other full-bodied red wine
juice of 3 oranges
1 tablespoon cornflour

Clean the fish and reserve the liver. Chop the oysters, anchovy fillets, liver and herbs and combine with the softened butter. Season with salt and a pinch of mace. Stuff the fish with this mixture and sew up the cavity to enclose the stuffing. Place in a baking tin. Pour in the wine and cover with a lid or foil. Cook in a moderate oven (180°C, 350°F, Gas Mark 4) for about 1¼ hours, until cooked, basting with the wine from time to time.

Place the fish on a hot serving dish. Add the orange juice to the cooking liquid. Moisten the cornflour with a little cold water, add to the pan and bring to the boil, stirring constantly. Season to taste and pour over the fish. *Makes about 12–16 servings.*

Oxford Sausages

This recipe dates from the Eighteenth Century and is traditionally made with equal quantities of pork and veal, so it is rather delicate in flavour.

225 g/8 oz lean pork
225 g/8 oz pie veal
225 g/8 oz shredded suet
100 g/4 oz fresh white breadcrumbs
½ teaspoon grated lemon rind
½ teaspoon freshly grated nutmeg
½ teaspoon dried sage
½ teaspoon dried thyme
½ teaspoon dried marjoram
1 teaspoon salt
¼ teaspoon black pepper
butter to fry

Finely mince the pork and veal with the suet. Add the breadcrumbs and moisten with a little water. Add the lemon rind, nutmeg, herbs, salt and pepper, and mix thoroughly. Form into sausage shapes with floured hands. Fry in butter for about 10 minutes, until golden brown on each side. *Makes about 16.*

Epping Sausages These are very similar but made with pork only, stuffed into skins, and usually a beaten egg is used to bind the mixture. Instead of being fried, they are cooked in links in boiling salted water for 15–20 minutes then served with pease pudding and onions fried the Cockney way, parboiled first.

Hereford Haslet

Recipes of this type are to be found in almost every region, sometimes called Aslett or Ayslet. This one is made mostly with offal.

450 g/1 lb belly of pork
1 kg/2 lb pig's liver
1 pig's heart
1 teaspoon salt
2 teaspoons pepper
2 teaspoons dried sage
6 tablespoons water
1 egg
100 g/4 oz fresh white breadcrumbs
caul, veil or flead
(available from the butcher, see note)

Mince the pork, liver and heart together twice until very fine. Mix with the remaining ingredients and form into an oval loaf. Wrap neatly in the caul, tucking the ends underneath. Place in a shallow ovenproof dish and bake in a moderately hot oven (190°C, 375°F, Gas Mark 5) for about 1–1¼ hours, until well browned. Leave in the dish for 10 minutes, then lift out and place on a plate to cool. *Makes 12 servings.*
Note This is the fatty membrane from a domestic animal's stomach (usually a pig) which is used to wrap the haslet.

Faggots

675 g/1½ lb pig's liver
225 g/8 oz fat pork
1 large onion, chopped
2 eggs
½ teaspoon freshly grated nutmeg
salt and pepper
225 g/8 oz dry white breadcrumbs
pig's caul, veil or flead
(available from the butcher)
150 ml/¼ pint beef stock

Soak the liver in salted water for 1 hour. Rinse and cook in fresh water until tender. Mince the liver, pork and onion together. Beat the eggs lightly with the nutmeg and seasoning to taste. Combine with the liver mixture and work in the breadcrumbs evenly. Wrap balls of the mixture in small squares of caul and arrange them side by side in a roasting tin with the joins underneath. Sprinkle over the stock and bake in a moderately hot oven (190°C, 375°F, Gas Mark 5) for 30–35 minutes, until well browned. *Makes 6 servings.*

Variation In other parts of the country the mixture is pressed into the roasting tin, covered with caul and then marked into squares for serving.

Black Pudding

The Midlands are particularly famous for their strong-flavoured black puddings. When a pig was slaughtered the blood was never wasted and when cooked it turns the pudding almost black in colour.

225 g/8 oz fresh white breadcrumbs
50 g/2 oz medium oatmeal
75 g/3 oz short-grain rice
50 g/2 oz barley
450 g/1 lb pork fat
450 g/1 lb onions
salt and pepper
½ teaspoon dried sage
600 ml/1 pint pig's blood

Soak the breadcrumbs in cold water then squeeze dry and place in a bowl. Put the oatmeal, rice and barley into a pan with water to cover. Bring to the boil and simmer until the grains are tender, about 20 minutes. Add extra boiling water if necessary but do not make the mixture too wet. It will be similar to porridge in consistency. Add to the breadcrumbs. Chop up the fat and onions. Stir into the mixture with plenty of seasoning, the sage and pig's blood. Turn into a greased baking tin and bake in a moderate oven (180°C, 350°F, Gas Mark 4) for about 1 hour, until firm.

To serve, cut slices and fry with the breakfast bacon. *Makes about 1.5 kg/3 lb.*

White Pudding

For those who prefer a paler colour and milder flavour, here is another traditional pudding, made without the pig's blood.

100 g/4 oz medium oatmeal
50 g/2 oz round-grain rice
50 g/2 oz barley
1·15 litres/2 pints milk and water
1 egg, beaten
225 g/8 oz pork fat
2 onions, chopped
salt and pepper
½ teaspoon dried sage

Mix and cook as for Black Pudding (see above). Sometimes the grain is cooked in a mixture of milk and water, if there is sufficient milk to spare. This pudding is smaller and needs slightly less cooking time. *Makes 675 g/1½ lb.*

Baked Suet Dumpling or Pudding

As in the North of England Yorkshire pudding accompanies roast meat, in the Midlands a joint is served with a baked suet pudding, cooked in the oven at the same time.

225 g/8 oz self-raising flour
pinch of salt
175 g/6 oz shredded suet
milk to mix

Sift the flour and salt into a bowl, stir in the shredded suet and sufficient milk to make a soft dough. Knead gently with floured hands and shape into a round about 2.5 cm/1 inch thick. Place on a greased baking tray and mark with a deep cross on top. Brush with milk and bake in a moderate oven (180°C, 350°F, Gas Mark 4) for 30–40 minutes, until well risen and golden brown. *Makes 6 servings.*

Melton Mowbray Pork Pies

Leicestershire is famous for its raised pork pies, the oldest named pies in England. Best eaten cold, they are traditionally moulded by hand in a round shape, called a 'coffyn' or 'coffer'. The best known Leicestershire pies come from Melton Mowbray.

Hot Water Crust Pastry
450 g/1 lb plain flour
pinch of salt
100 g/4 oz lard
300 ml/$\frac{1}{2}$ pint hot water
beaten egg to brush
Filling
1 kg/2 lb shoulder of pork
1 teaspoon salt
$\frac{1}{2}$ teaspoon cayenne pepper
$\frac{1}{4}$ teaspoon freshly ground black pepper
$\frac{1}{4}$ teaspoon ground allspice
1 teaspoon gelatine

First make the pastry coffyns. Sift the flour and salt into a warmed bowl (to prevent the hot water from cooling too quickly) and make a well in the centre. Bring the lard to the boil in the water, stirring to make sure the lard is completely melted, and pour into the dry ingredients. Mix the pastry quickly, first with a wooden spoon, then with the hands, until smooth and free from cracks. Divide the pastry into four and shape three-quarters of each portion quickly, raising it round four floured (450-g/1-lb) jam jars, while still warm. Keep the remaining pastry in a polythene bag and allow the pastry coffyns to set in the refrigerator until firm. Carefully ease off the jam jars and place the pastry cases on a baking tray. Shape the remaining pastry to make four lids.

To make the filling, bone and dice the meat. Use the bones and trimmings to make a strong stock. Toss the meat in the mixed seasonings and spice and pack into the pastry cases. Cover with the pie lids, dampen the edges and pinch to make a standing edge, or cut in turret fashion. Brush the tops with beaten egg and make a small steam vent. Bake in a hot oven (220°C, 425°F, Gas Mark 7) for 30 minutes, then reduce the heat to moderate (180°C, 350°F, Gas Mark 4) for a further 1$\frac{1}{2}$–2 hours. Cool. Dissolve the gelatine in 1 tablespoon very hot water, stir in 6 tablespoons strong stock and pour into the cold pies until it comes level with the steam vent. Serve cold. *Makes 4. Illustrated left.*

Left
Melton Mowbray is famed for the quality of its pork pies, and in this part of the Midlands they are still traditionally served at Sunday breakfast.

Beef in a Blanket

In some counties this recipe is known as Beefy Toad but the title given above is perhaps more appetising and descriptive.

Meatballs
350 g/12 oz minced beef
50 g/2 oz fresh white breadcrumbs
1 large onion, grated
1 tablespoon sweet chutney
2 teaspoons Worcestershire sauce
¼ teaspoon dried mixed herbs
salt and pepper
Batter
100 g/4 oz plain flour
½ teaspoon salt
1 egg, separated
300 ml/½ pint milk

Combine all the ingredients for the meatballs together, and form into eight balls. Arrange in a shallow ovenproof dish.

To make the batter, sift the flour and salt into a bowl, add the egg yolk and half the milk. Beat until smooth, then stir in the rest of the milk. Whisk the egg white until almost stiff then fold into the batter. Pour over the meatballs and bake in a hot oven (220°C, 425°F, Gas Mark 7) for about 40 minutes, until well risen and golden brown. *Makes 4 servings.*

Hunting Beef

In Victorian times an enormous round of beef was pickled and cooked in this way, to be served at breakfast before the hunt, or packed in sandwiches to be taken out tucked into a convenient pocket.

2.75-kg/6-lb joint of silverside
or brisket of beef
350 g/12 oz salt
(grated block salt if possible)
7 g/¼ oz saltpetre
25 g/1 oz soft brown sugar
2 bay leaves, crumbled
¼ teaspoon ground mace
2 cloves
300 ml/½ pint mild or light ale

Place the beef in a large bowl. Mix the other dry ingredients and rub into the beef. Leave in a cool place for four days, rubbing the beef every day with the brine mixture. Leave for a further week to ten days, turning the meat daily. When the meat is sufficiently salted, rinse under cold water and place in a pan with the ale. Add sufficient water to cover. Bring to the boil and simmer for 4½–5 hours, until quite tender. Either serve hot with freshly boiled floury potatoes, onions and a green vegetable, or allow to get cold and serve with salads or in sandwiches. *Makes 20 servings.*

Quorn Bacon Roll

This famous hunt has given its name to a very hearty dish which is traditionally served to the hunt servants.

450 g/1 lb self-raising flour
1 teaspoon salt
225 g/8 oz shredded suet
1 tablespoon chopped parsley
Filling
2 onions
450 g/1 lb lean bacon rashers, derinded
2 teaspoons dried sage
salt and pepper

Sift the flour and salt into a bowl. Stir in the suet and add sufficient cold water to make a firm dough. Roll out on a floured surface to a rectangle 1–1.5 cm/½–¾ inch thick. Finely chop the onions. Lay the bacon rashers on top of the pastry and sprinkle with the sage, onion and seasoning. Roll up like a Swiss roll and wrap in a sheet of greased greaseproof paper or foil, folding and crimping the edges to seal. Place in a steamer over a pan of boiling water and cook for 2–2½ hours, making sure the pan does not boil dry. Remove the wrapping and turn the roll on to a hot serving dish. Sprinkle with the parsley and serve with cooked vegetables and plenty of good gravy. *Makes 6–8 servings.*

Ham Stuffed with Apricots

Juicy 'Moor Park' apricots were once used with sweetcured ham to make this Oxfordshire dish, but any large firm apricots would do as well.

2.25–2.75-kg/5–6-lb joint of gammon
225 g/8 oz firm apricots
100 g/4 oz fresh white breadcrumbs
50 g/2 oz flaked almonds
100 g/4 oz demerara sugar
1 tablespoon treacle
675 g/1½ lb plain flour
cloves and blanched almonds to decorate

Remove the bone from the gammon. Halve the apricots and take out the stones. Put the fruit in a saucepan with 2 tablespoons water and heat gently until the juices begin to run. Remove from the heat and stir in the breadcrumbs, almonds and half the sugar. Pack this stuffing into the cavity in the joint. Tie with string to make a neat shape. Rub the treacle all over the surface and press in the rest of the sugar.

Put the flour into a bowl and add sufficient water to make a very stiff dough. Mould around the gammon, to enclose completely, moisten the edges and seal together very firmly. Place in a roasting tin and cook in a cool oven (150°C, 300°F, Gas Mark 2) for 3 hours. Take from the oven and leave to cool in the crust. When cold, break off the crust and discard it. Decorate the gammon with cloves and blanched almonds. *Makes 10–12 servings.*

Note Instead of adding flaked almonds to the stuffing, 2 or 3 blanched kernels from the apricot stones were often used.

Jugged Hare with Forcemeat Balls

The original recipe meant exactly what it said; the hare was placed in a tall earthenware jug which in its turn was placed in a deep pan of boiling water until the meat was cooked. If possible red wine was used in the cooking and any blood from the hare added to the sauce at the end.

1 hare, jointed
50 g/2 oz seasoned flour
dripping to fry
1 large onion, chopped
6 tablespoons red wine
2 tablespoons redcurrant jelly
1 bouquet garni
Forcemeat Balls
liver from the hare
2 rashers streaky bacon, derinded
100 g/4 oz shredded suet
175 g/6 oz fresh white breadcrumbs
1 tablespoon chopped parsley
1 teaspoon dried mixed herbs
finely grated rind of ½ lemon
2 eggs, beaten
salt and pepper
pinch of ground mace

Remove all the flesh from the hare portions. Wash and dry the meat. Put the bones and head in a large pan, just cover with water and simmer for 1½ hours. Cool slightly. Coat the meat in seasoned flour and fry gently in 50 g/2 oz dripping. Add the onion and continue to fry until the meat is golden brown all over. Transfer the meat and onion to a large ovenproof casserole. Add the remaining seasoned flour to the fat left in the pan and stir until smooth. Gradually add sufficient strained stock from the bones, stirring to make a slightly thickened gravy. Mix in the wine and redcurrant jelly and when the jelly has melted, pour over the meat. Add the bouquet garni, cover and cook in a moderate oven (160°C, 325°F, Gas Mark 3) for 3 hours.

Meanwhile, make the forcemeat balls. Cook the liver in boiling water for 5 minutes. Drain and break up with a fork. Chop the bacon, add to the liver with the remaining ingredients. Form into small balls and fry in hot dripping until golden brown all over. Alternatively, place in an ovenproof dish with a little dripping and bake in the oven with the hare for 30 minutes, basting and turning them occasionally.

Remove the bouquet garni from the hare mixture and adjust the seasoning if necessary. Serve with the forcemeat balls and potatoes baked in their jackets. *Makes 8 servings.*

Staffordshire Game Pie

This pie may be made with any feathered game, particularly that which has been damaged by shot and is unsuitable for roasting.

1 pheasant or 2 partridges or 2 pigeons
salt and pepper
225 g/8 oz shortcrust or puff pastry
(made with 225 g/8 oz flour, etc.)
milk to brush
Forcemeat
225 g/8 oz fresh white breadcrumbs
75 g/3 oz shredded suet
½ teaspoon dried thyme
1 teaspoon chopped parsley
1 lemon
1 egg

Prepare and clean the birds and cut into portions. Place in a pan, cover with cold water and bring to the boil. Drain the portions, rinse with cold water and return to the pan. Add 600 ml/1 pint cold water and seasoning, bring to the boil, cover and simmer for 1 hour.

Mix the breadcrumbs, suet and herbs in a bowl. Grate the rind of half the lemon and add to the breadcrumb mixture. Squeeze the lemon and stir the juice with the egg into the forcemeat until it binds together. Form into small balls and add to the pan with the game. Cook for a further 1 hour. Transfer to a 1.75-litre/3-pint pie dish. Roll out the pastry on a floured board and use to cover the pie, having first lined the rim of the dish with a strip of pastry. Moisten, seal well and decorate with pastry trimmings. Brush with milk and bake in a moderately hot oven (200°C, 400°F, Gas Mark 6) for 30 minutes, until golden brown. *Makes 4 servings. Illustrated on the title page.*

Left and Above
Bread making in the Midlands is a time-honoured art. Harvest Triple Plait (left) has the professional touch of a master baker, while homely Cottage Loaves (right) still go to make up many a ploughman's lunch (above).

Cottage Loaves

675 g/$1\frac{1}{2}$ lb plain flour
15 g/$\frac{1}{2}$ oz salt
15 g/$\frac{1}{2}$ oz lard
25 g/1 oz fresh yeast
1 teaspoon sugar
450 ml/$\frac{3}{4}$ pint warm water
beaten egg to brush

Sift the flour and salt into a bowl. Rub in the fat. Cream the yeast with the sugar and gradually blend in the water. Leave in a warm place for about 10 minutes, until frothy. Add the yeast liquid to the dry ingredients and mix to a firm dough. Turn out on a lightly floured surface and knead until firm and elastic. Return to the bowl, cover and leave in a warm place until double in size. Knead lightly and divide into three equal portions. Shape two of these into rounds and place on greased baking trays. Divide the remaining dough in half and form each piece into a round. Brush the two larger rounds with salted water and place a smaller round on each one. Press the floured handle of a wooden spoon right down the centre of each loaf to the baking tray. Cover and prove in a warm place until almost double in size. Brush with beaten egg, bake in the centre of a hot oven (230°C, 450°F, Gas Mark 8) for 5 minutes, then reduce to 200°C, 400°F, Gas Mark 6 for a further 25–30 minutes. The loaves should be golden brown, crisp on the outside and sound hollow when tapped on the base with the knuckles. *Makes 2. Illustrated left.*

Pickled Onions

Top and tail small pickling or silverskin onions. Try not to cut away too much flesh or the onions will come apart. Place them unpeeled in a bowl, pour over boiling water, leave 1 minute then drain and cover with cold water. Remove the skins, keeping the onions under the water. Drain well and sprinkle generously with salt. Allow to stand for 12 hours or overnight. Rinse with cold water, drain and dry. Pack the onions tightly into jars. Prepare a spiced vinegar in the proportion of 1.15 litres/2 pints vinegar to 50 g/2 oz mixed pickling spices (tied in a muslin bag) and 50 g/2 oz granulated sugar. Bring to the boil and simmer for 5 minutes. Remove the spices and pour the vinegar over the onions to cover them well. Seal the jars tightly and leave for at least 3 weeks before eating.

Ploughman's Lunch

A sensible custom which had almost died out and has recently been restored is the serving of a simple meal at lunchtime in almost every public house. It consists of freshly baked bread (often in the shape of a miniature cottage loaf) with a wedge of cheese and a generous helping of pickled onions. This was the meal which most country labourers took to work to eat at midday with a glass of beer. Illustrated on preceding page.

Harvest Triple Plait

25 g/1 oz fresh yeast
450 ml/¾ pint warm water
675 g/1½ lb wholewheat flour
1 tablespoon salt
15 g/½ oz butter
1 tablespoon soft brown sugar
cracked wheat to sprinkle

Cream the yeast and gradually blend in the water. Leave in a warm place for 10 minutes, or until frothy. Mix the flour and salt in a bowl. Rub in the fat and stir in the sugar. Add the yeast liquid and mix to a firm dough, adding extra flour if the mixture is too sticky to handle. Turn on to a lightly floured surface and knead thoroughly for 5–10 minutes until smooth and elastic. Shape the dough into a ball, cover and allow to rise until double in size. Knead lightly and cut in half. Divide one half into three strands and roll each strand out between the hands until about 50 cm/20 inches long. Plait the strands together, dampen and seal the ends. Divide the second piece of dough into two parts, one slightly larger than the other. Repeat the rolling and plaiting process to make two more plaits with strands about 40 cm/16 inches and 35 cm/14 inches long respectively. Place the large plait on a greased baking tray, brush with salted water and put the medium plait on top, making sure that the two stick firmly together. Brush again with salted water, and top with the smallest plait. Brush all over with salted water and sprinkle with cracked wheat. Cover and leave until double in size. Bake in a hot oven (230°C, 450°F, Gas Mark 8) for 35–45 minutes. *Illustrated on preceding pages.*

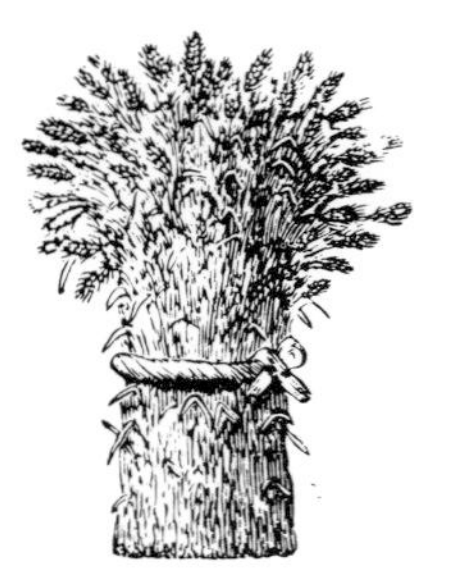

Gloucestershire Melted Cheese

Lay thin slices of Double Gloucester cheese in a buttered ovenproof dish, spreading each slice with a little mild mustard. Repeat two or three layers. Pour in sufficient ale to just cover. Place the dish uncovered in a moderate oven (180°C, 350°F, Gas Mark 4) until the cheese begins to melt. Meanwhile, toast thick slices of wholemeal bread, moisten the toast slightly with a tablespoon or two of hot ale and spoon over the melted cheese.

Stilton Savoury

Toast thick slices of wholemeal bread. Cover each slice with chopped watercress, thinly sliced ripe William pears and slices of Stilton cheese. Arrange in a buttered ovenproof dish and place in a moderate oven (180°C, 350°F, Gas Mark 4) for 5 minutes. Top with a sprinkling of cayenne pepper and serve as a savoury.

Bedfordshire Clanger

A big family meal could be boiled in a cloth in the old-fashioned cauldron and have a savoury filling at one end and a sweet filling at the other. Children loved it for its surprise element!

675 g/1½ lb self-raising flour
pinch of salt
350 g/12 oz shredded suet
Savoury Fillings
450 g/1 lb stewed steak, kidney and onion mixture
or
450 g/1 lb cooked pork, apple and onion mixture
Sweet Fillings
225 g/8 oz sliced cooking apple, 50 g/2 oz sugar and 50 g/2 oz dried fruit
or
350 g/12 oz mincemeat
or
225 g/8 oz ripe apricots and 100 g/4 oz chopped dates

Sift the flour and salt into a bowl. Stir in the suet and mix to a stiff dough with a little cold water. Knead lightly, reserve a very small piece of the dough and roll out the remainder to make a large rectangle. Roll out the reserved pastry to make a strip long enough to divide the pastry rectangle into two equal parts. Spread one part with a savoury mixture and the other with a sweet filling. Roll over gently, Swiss roll fashion, moisten and seal the ends. Mark the roll to indicate the fillings. Wrap in greased greaseproof paper or foil, leaving space for expansion. Crimp the wrapping to seal and steam for 1½ hours. Open the package and serve the savoury side with vegetables and plenty of good gravy. Re-wrap the remainder and return to the steamer to keep hot. When required, serve with a sweet sauce or custard. *Makes 4 savoury servings and 4 sweet servings.*

Frying Herbs

Sorrel is an old English herb, still cultivated abroad but not so often seen here nowadays. Spinach is a good substitute if a little lemon juice is added.

450 g/1 lb fresh young sorrel or spinach
50 g/2 oz parsley
1 lettuce heart
1 bunch spring onions
50 g/2 oz butter
salt and pepper

Trim and wash the sorrel, parsley, lettuce and onions. Chop roughly. Melt the butter in a saucepan over gentle heat, add the prepared greens and season well. Shake the pan occasionally until the contents become moist and steamy then cover tightly and simmer for about 20 minutes, until very tender. Serve with fried liver or ham and eggs. *Makes 4 servings.*

Pail Dinner

This was a speciality of the narrow boats which plied our canals throughout the Midlands at one time. Facilities for cooking were severely limited by the space aboard. Dinner for the bargee and his family could be cooked in a large pail over a small flame and this is how it was done.

A large earthenware jar was put in a pail or bucket containing water to about half the jar's depth. The bottom of the jar was filled with meat, sometimes ham or rabbit, and root vegetables, and water or stock added to cover. The water surrounding the jar was then brought to the boil. Over the simmering meat went a lid of suet crust which, when partly cooked, was in turn covered with sliced potatoes. Another layer of crust was added and finally some sliced cooking apples. The whole was covered with a cloth and simmered for a further 2 hours. This provided a complete meal for everyone, taking all morning to cook with a minimum of attention. The pudding at the top was removed and kept hot while the broth, meat and vegetables were consumed first.

Blackberry Curd

This recipe comes from a household book kept by a countrywoman over 200 years ago, preceded by the following lines:

'Why has bounteous Nature given,
with full and generous hands,
Fruits of the heath and hedgerow,
and flowers of the dells and sands,
All free to man for the taking,
that he may eat and live?
So take and use them wisely,
while grateful thanks ye give.'

1 cooking apple, peeled
450 g/1 lb ripe blackberries
225 g/8 oz castor sugar
2 eggs, beaten
100 g/4 oz butter
finely grated rind and juice of 1 lemon

Core and chop the apple. Place in a pan with the blackberries. Crush with a wooden spoon, then cook gently until soft. Press through a sieve to remove the pips. Put the pulp in the top of a double saucepan with the sugar, eggs, butter, lemon rind and juice. Stir constantly over simmering water until the mixture thickens. Pour into small pots and allow to cool. Cover and label when cold. The curd will keep in a cool place for about 2 months if the pots are well sealed. Use up quickly once opened. *Makes about 675 g/$1\frac{1}{2}$ lb. Illustrated right.*

Banbury Cakes

A shop in Banbury claims to have been selling these cakes since 1638, and they were certainly mentioned by Ben Jonson at the beginning of the Seventeenth Century.

100 g/4 oz butter, softened
100 g/4 oz finely chopped mixed peel
100 g/4 oz sultanas or seedless raisins
1 teaspoon ground cinnamon
1 teaspoon ground allspice
50 g/2 oz clear honey
450 g/1 lb prepared puff pastry
milk to brush
castor sugar to sprinkle

First make the filling. Cream the butter until light and fluffy. Blend in the peel, sultanas, spices and honey. Roll out the pastry thinly on a floured surface and cut into 10-cm/4-inch rounds with a biscuit cutter. Spoon a little heap of the spice mixture in the centre of half the pastry rounds. Moisten the edges and cover with the remaining pastry rounds, sealing the edges well together. Flatten slightly with a rolling pin. Make a small slit in the top to allow steam to escape. Brush the tops with milk and sprinkle with sugar. Place on dampened baking trays and bake in a hot oven (220°C, 425°F, Gas Mark 7) for 15 minutes. Cool on a wire rack. The cakes may be eaten hot or cold. *Makes 10–12. Illustrated right.*

Banbury Pie

225 g/8 oz shortcrust pastry
(made with 225 g/8 oz flour, etc.)
75 g/3 oz ground rice
600 ml/1 pint milk
pared rind of $\frac{1}{2}$ lemon
4 eggs
75 g/3 oz butter, melted
2 tablespoons castor sugar
1 tablespoon currants

Roll out the pastry and use to line a 25-cm/10-inch flan dish or ring. Blend the rice with a little of the milk until smooth. Place the remainder of the milk in a saucepan with the lemon rind and bring to the boil. Remove the rind and stir in the rice mixture. Heat gently, stirring all the time, until just thickened. Cool. Beat together the eggs, butter and sugar, and mix these with the cooled rice mixture. Pour into the pastry case, sprinkle the currants over the top and bake in a moderate oven (180°C, 350°F, Gas Mark 4) for about 45 minutes, until the pastry is cooked and the filling golden brown. *Makes 6 servings. Illustrated right.*

Mansfield Gooseberry Pie

This unusual fruit pie is made of hot water crust pastry (see page 79) exactly as for a pork pie, so it is a raised pie filled with fruit and sugar instead of meat. The gooseberries must be dry and firm, and packed well into the pastry case (without adding any liquid). The pie must be firm enough to cut into neat wedges, and it is always sold at the annual Gooseberry Pie Fair in Mansfield.

Right
'Ride a Cock-Horse to Banbury Cross'. So begins a children's nursery rhyme, and most children would be thrilled by this Banbury tea, offering the traditional Banbury Cakes, Banbury Pie and brown bread and butter spread with Blackberry Curd.

SNAP
A CAPITAL ROUND GAME
JOHN JAQUES & SON
Celebrated Stories.

Ashover Pancakes

This very old recipe is still made in the Nottinghamshire village of Linby, to record the massacre of Danish invaders on an Ash Wednesday in Saxon times. Some people believe these pancakes are the ancestors of today's Shrove Tuesday pancakes.

450 g/1 lb plain flour
½ teaspoon bicarbonate of soda
1 teaspoon cream of tartar
4 teaspoons baking powder
50 g/2 oz shredded suet
2 eggs, beaten
fat or oil to deep fry

Sift the flour, bicarbonate of soda, cream of tartar and baking powder into a bowl. Stir in the suet and add the eggs. Mix to a firm dough. Divide into balls the size of a walnut and fry, a few at a time, in deep hot fat or oil until golden brown. Drain well and place in an ovenproof dish. Heat through in a cool oven (150°C, 300°F, Gas Mark 2) for a few minutes until softened. Serve hot with jam or syrup. *Makes 6 servings.*

Quakers' Chocolate Pudding

In the counties where cocoa was first manufactured from the bean, chocolate has always been used in puddings and cakes, though this is not traditional elsewhere.

100 g/4 oz plain or bitter chocolate
150 ml/¼ pint milk
75 g/3 oz butter
100 g/4 oz fresh white breadcrumbs
100 g/4 oz castor sugar
few drops of vanilla essence
2 eggs, separated

Grate the chocolate. Warm the milk and butter and when melted stir in the chocolate. Add the breadcrumbs and cook gently for 10 minutes, stirring from time to time to prevent the mixture from sticking. Remove from the heat and cool slightly. Beat the sugar, vanilla essence and egg yolks. Whisk the egg whites until stiff and fold into the mixture. Turn into a buttered 1-litre/1¾-pint pudding basin. Cover with buttered greaseproof paper or foil with a pleat in the centre and tie on firmly. Stand the basin in a saucepan and add sufficient boiling water to come halfway up the sides of the basin. Cover and steam for 50 minutes, adding more water if necessary. Serve with whipped cream. *Makes 4 servings.*

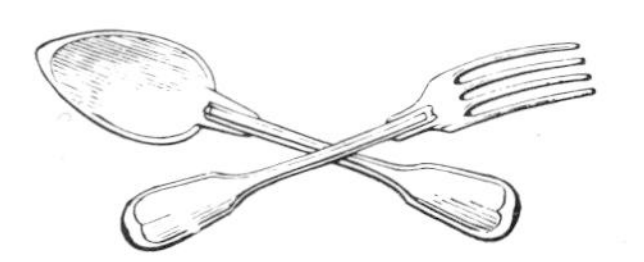

Rockings Pudding

In Bledworth Church, on the wall above the font, hangs a 'Register of Rockings'. Each year on the last Sunday in February, the latest baby boy to be baptised is placed near the altar in a beautiful cradle decorated with flowers, and 'rocked' (usually by the Bishop). This pudding is always served at lunch afterwards.

50 g/2 oz butter
50 g/2 oz castor sugar
1 egg, beaten
100 g/4 oz self-raising flour
milk to mix
4 tablespoons strawberry jam

Cream the butter and sugar until fluffy. Gradually beat in the egg then fold in the flour and enough milk to make a soft dropping consistency. Spread the jam in the base of a well-greased 1-litre/1¾-pint pudding basin and spoon the pudding mixture on top. Cover with greased greaseproof paper or foil with a pleat in the centre, and tie on firmly. Place in a saucepan and add boiling water to come halfway up the sides of the basin. Steam for 1½ hours, adding more water when necessary. Turn out to serve. *Makes 4 servings.*

Coventry Godcakes

These delicacies have been made by pastry cooks in the district around Coventry since Lady Godiva's day. They are traditional New Year fare when godparents give them to their godchildren for good luck.

675 g/1½ lb prepared puff pastry
450 g/1 lb mincemeat
1 egg white
sifted icing sugar to sprinkle

Roll out the pastry to about 3 mm/⅛ inch thick and cut into matching triangular shapes. Place a spoonful of mincemeat in the centre of one pastry triangle, top with another triangle, moisten the edges and press well together. Repeat with the remaining pastry triangles. Make 3 small slits in the top of each cake, place on a dampened baking tray, then bake in a hot oven (220°C, 425°F, Gas Mark 7) for about 15 minutes, until well risen and golden. Meanwhile, whisk the egg white until frothy. When the cakes are cooked, brush the tops with egg white and sprinkle with icing sugar. Return to the oven for 3 minutes, then cool on a wire rack. *Makes about 15.*

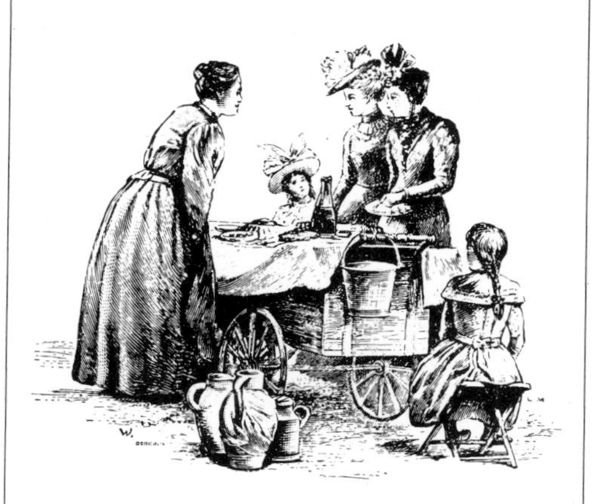

Nottingham Goosefair Gingerbreads

175 g/6 oz self-raising flour
2 teaspoons ground ginger
75 g/3 oz butter
175 g/6 oz castor sugar
beaten egg to mix

Sift the flour and ginger into a bowl. Rub in the butter and stir in the sugar. Add sufficient beaten egg to make a stiff dough. Knead until smooth. Pinch off small pieces and roll in the hands to the size of walnuts. Place well apart on ungreased baking trays and bake in a moderate oven (160°C, 325°F, Gas Mark 3) for about 20–25 minutes, until pale golden. *Makes about 18.*

Shrewsbury Cakes

225 g/8 oz butter
225 g/8 oz castor sugar
1 egg, beaten
grated rind and juice of 1 lemon
4 tablespoons double cream
350 g/12 oz self-raising flour, sifted

Slightly warm the butter and beat with the sugar until light and fluffy. Gradually beat in the egg, lemon rind and juice and the cream. Add the flour and mix to a soft dough. Knead well and allow to rest in a cool place for 1 hour. Roll out on a floured surface to a thickness of about 5 mm/¼ inch. Cut into 6-cm/2½-inch rounds with a biscuit cutter. Place on a greased baking tray and bake in a moderately hot oven (190°C, 375°F, Gas Mark 5) for 15–20 minutes. *Makes about 24.*

Gloucester Tarts

225 g/8 oz shortcrust pastry
(made with 225 g/8 oz flour, etc.)
2 tablespoons raspberry jam
50 g/2 oz butter
50 g/2 oz castor sugar
1 egg, beaten
25 g/1 oz ground rice
50 g/2 oz ground almonds
few drops of almond essence
glacé icing to decorate

Roll out the pastry thinly and use to line 12 bun tins. Put a little raspberry jam into each tart. Cream the butter and sugar together until light and fluffy. Gradually add the egg. Stir in the ground rice and almonds with the almond essence. Put about 2 teaspoons of this almond mixture on top of the jam in each tart and bake in a moderate oven (180°C, 350°F, Gas Mark 4) for 25 minutes. When cold, run a little plain glacé icing over the tops. *Makes 12.*

The West Country

Land of ancient legends and lush green fields, the furthermost tip of England stretches out westwards into the Atlantic. It lies dreaming still, almost a kingdom apart, cradled by the swell of the warm Gulf Stream which makes it so fruitful and fair. In this region food is abundant . . . the red earth of Devon and parts of Cornwall produces marvellous grazing for cattle. Clotted cream, the pride of the West, is the result of their enormous yield of rich milk.

This cream is never stinted in cooking, even in a humble household, and it is piled on to yeasted scones, called splits, with a lavish hand. Cream teas in Devon and Cornwall are a tourist's most eagerly awaited treat. Even the sudden storms which blow up around the treacherous coast have given their name to a teatime treat; 'Thunder and Lightning' is bread liberally spread with black treacle and clotted cream.

Shoals of mackerel and pilchards are the traditional catch, and fishing is an important industry. Cornwall is famous for its 'Star Gazers'; pies which enclose the fish in a golden pastry jacket. The pastry is made with freshly churned butter and lard from the 'orchard' pigs, who root happily among cider-apple trees in the orchards for which the region is renowned. These pigs often got helplessly drunk on fermenting windfalls and had to sleep it off like old topers in the village tavern.

Coming eastwards towards the River Avon and the noble cities of Bristol and Bath, the emphasis is more on good baking, in all its forms, on pork, and on cider. This is the supreme cider country. It produces small varieties of cider apple, with strange names such as Slapmagirdle and Hangydown; apples that have been used to make a delectable and sometimes highly alcoholic drink since time out of mind.

The West is rich in folk lore, and perpetuates the pagan rites of wassailing the apple trees to ensure a good crop. Fruit trees seem to have mystified even the Druids, with their inexplicable habit of cropping well one year, then bearing no fruit the next without apparent reason.

The toe of Britain is both fruitful and fair.

Fish

The great Cornish toast of 'fish, tin and copper' rightly puts fish as the prime source of this region's prosperity. Its lonely coves used to invite smugglers by night while the fierce tides have driven many a helpless ship on to the rocks by day. Fishing is a perilous business off the toe of Britain, but danger has never deterred the hardy West Country folk.

Star Gazers

There are various pasties and pies made with pilchards, mackerel and even herrings, which are traditional fare in Cornwall. Sometimes the names are confused, but these authentic recipes show exactly how they differ. In every case the fishes' heads are used as part of the recipe and these are the 'star gazers'. For reasons of economy the heads were not discarded because they contain much of the delicious juices and oils of the fish which the frugal Cornish folk would be loth to waste.

Star-Gazing Pasties

The great fish markets of Cornwall were not complete without stalls selling these pasties, often quite enormous in size. Sometimes a single pasty cooked by a local baker would contain as many as two dozen pilchards.

This is how they are made. An oblong of flaky or puff pastry is rolled out long enough to 'put to bed' two dozen fish side by side with their heads sticking out, and wide enough to fold up and make a 'top cover'. The fish are gutted, the tails removed, and the cavities filled with chopped onion, fresh herbs and pats of butter. They are then laid side by side on their pastry bed and the other half of the oblong brought up and tucked in under their chins, so to speak. The pastry is marked between the fish so that when this huge pasty is baked and ready to serve, a whole fish in its pastry blanket can easily be cut off. Sometimes these pasties are known locally as 'swaddled pilchards'.

Star-Gazing Pie

For this you need a fairly deep round pie dish, large enough to take six cleaned pilchards. Place a pie funnel in the centre and arrange the tails of the fish curling up the sides of the funnel, with their heads radiating out to the edge. Fill the spaces between the fish with sliced hard-boiled egg, sprinkle well with salt and pepper and cover the dish with 225 g/8 oz shortcrust pastry (made with 225 g/8 oz flour, etc.), allowing the fish heads to poke up through it. Glaze the pastry with beaten egg and bake in a moderately hot oven (200°C, 400°F, Gas Mark 6) for 20 minutes, then reduce the heat to moderate (180°C, 350°F, Gas Mark 4) for a further 10–15 minutes, until the pie is a rich golden brown. *Makes 6 servings.*

Note The heads can easily be broken off and discarded when serving.

Star-Gazy Pie

6 small herring or mackerel
salt and pepper
2 tablespoons chopped parsley
100 g/4 oz dry white breadcrumbs
3 rashers streaky bacon, derinded
1 tablespoon white vinegar
4 eggs, beaten
225 g/8 oz prepared puff or flaky pastry
1 sprig of parsley

Remove the heads and tails from the fish and reserve the heads. Clean, split and bone them, lay flat and season both sides. Scatter over the parsley and roll each fish up, skin side outwards. Put half the breadcrumbs in a well buttered 1.5-litre/2½-pint pie dish, arrange the fish rolls on this and cover with the remaining breadcrumbs. Place the bacon on top. Whisk the vinegar into the beaten eggs and pour into the dish. Roll out the pastry to form a lid, dampen the edges and seal well to the dish, making six steam vents around the outside. Bake in a hot oven (220°C, 425°F, Gas Mark 7) for 20 minutes. Place the fish heads over the steam vents then reduce to 190°C, 375°F, Gas Mark 5 for a further 25 minutes, until the pastry is well browned. To serve, garnish with a sprig of parsley. *Makes 6 servings.* *Illustrated on page 95.*

Tiddy Eel

Conger eel is caught off the shores of Cornwall and sometimes the fish is of tremendous size and used to be salted for winter use. This recipe is for fresh conger eel, cooked with potatoes in cider. For this reason in some places it is called Tiddly Eel, but tiddy does in fact mean potato in common Cornish parlance.

450 g/1 lb conger eel
675 g/$1\frac{1}{2}$ lb potatoes, sliced
1 medium onion, chopped
450 ml/$\frac{3}{4}$ pint dry cider
salt and pepper
25 g/1 oz butter
25 g/1 oz flour
150 ml/$\frac{1}{4}$ pint milk
1 tablespoon chopped parsley

Skin, bone and cut the eel into strips. Place in an ovenproof casserole with the potato and onion, pour over the cider and season well. Cover and cook in a moderate oven (180°C, 350°F, Gas Mark 4) for 45 minutes.

Melt the butter in a saucepan, stir in the flour and cook for 1 minute. Gradually add the strained liquid from cooking the fish and the milk. Bring to the boil, stirring constantly. Cook for 3 minutes and season to taste. Serve portions of the fish mixture masked with sauce and sprinkled with parsley. *Makes 4 servings.*

Fried Mackerel with Gooseberry Sauce

6 medium mackerel, cleaned
100 g/4 oz butter
Sauce
225 g/8 oz gooseberries
150 ml/$\frac{1}{4}$ pint water
40 g/$1\frac{1}{2}$ oz butter
40 g/$1\frac{1}{2}$ oz flour
600 ml/1 pint milk
pinch of freshly grated nutmeg
salt and pepper

Fry the fish in the butter for about 5–7 minutes on each side, according to size. Use two frying pans if necessary. Meanwhile, make the sauce. Stew the gooseberries in the water until soft then sieve, or liquidise and sieve, to remove the pips. Melt the butter in a clean saucepan and stir in the flour. Cook for 1 minute. Gradually add the milk and bring to the boil, stirring constantly. Add the gooseberry pulp, a little nutmeg and seasoning to taste. Cook for 2 minutes. Place in a sauceboat and hand separately with the mackerel. *Makes 6 servings.* *Illustrated overleaf.*

Above
Star-Gazy Pie
Left
A lucky night's catch for a Cornish fisherman could mean for his family any of the following traditional West Country dishes: Fried Mackerel with Gooseberry Sauce, Mussels with Saffron, or a tureen of Cornish Crab Soup, swirled with thick cream.

Cornish Crab Soup

1 litre/1¾ pints chicken stock
75 g/3 oz long-grain rice
1 litre/1¾ pints milk
salt and pepper
¼ teaspoon freshly grated nutmeg
1 medium crab, cooked
150 ml/¼ pint double cream

Place the chicken stock and rice in a large saucepan and bring to the boil. Stir well and simmer for 10 minutes. Add the milk, seasoning and nutmeg, bring back to the boil then simmer until the rice is soft. Take the flesh from the crab and chop the white crabmeat. Pound the dark crabmeat, mix into the soup and press through a sieve, or liquidise until smooth. Return to the rinsed out pan and add the white crabmeat. Adjust seasoning and bring to boiling point. Stir in the cream, swirling it over the top, and reheat but do not allow to boil. *Makes 8 servings. Illustrated left.*

Mussels with Saffron

Mussels are so popular in France that they are frequently served in small restaurants with fried potatoes – 'Moules Pommes Frites'. Oddly enough the more elaborate way of cooking them with cider and saffron is Cornish and often superior to the French 'Moules Marinières' using white wine.

1.15 litres / 2 pints mussels
1 medium onion, chopped
generous pinch of saffron strands
1 bay leaf
2 sprigs of parsley
150 ml/¼ pint dry cider
25 g/1 oz butter
1 large leek, sliced
1 clove garlic, chopped
salt and pepper

Scrub the mussels, scrape off beards and discard any shells which are not tightly closed. Place them in a large saucepan with the onion, saffron strands, bay leaf, parsley and cider. Cover and cook for 10 minutes, or until the shells open. Remove from the heat, strain off the cooking liquid and reserve for the sauce. Keep the cooked mussels hot.

Melt the butter in a clean pan and use to fry the leek and garlic until soft. Stir in the reserved mussel liquid and bring to the boil, stirring constantly. Add the mussels to the sauce and season to taste. Reheat to boiling point and serve in soup plates with crusty white bread. *Makes 4 servings. Illustrated left.*

Meat

Because fish is so plentiful, certain great meat recipes of the West Country are often overlooked. The following are representative of those using lamb, mutton, pork and beef.

Squab Pie

The old name for pigeon, squab, is still used to describe a famous West Country pie which is nowadays usually made entirely with mutton or lamb. The strong flavour and texture of mutton does rather resemble that of a plump pigeon breast, especially when combined with onion and tart cooking apples. This recipe includes both mutton and pigeon.

450 g/1 lb neck of mutton or lamb cutlets
2 large tart cooking apples
1 large onion
4 pigeon breasts
salt and pepper
pinch of ground allspice
225 g/8 oz shortcrust pastry
(made with 225 g/8 oz flour, etc.)
milk to brush

Bone the cutlets and use the bones and trimmings to make 300 ml/½ pint strong stock. Peel, core and slice the apples and finely chop the onion. Pack a 1.5-litre/2½-pint pie dish carefully with layers of meat, breast of pigeon, onion and apple around a pie funnel. Season well between the layers. Add the allspice to the stock and pour into the pie dish. Roll out the pastry to make a lid, dampen the edges and seal well to the rim of the dish. Cut a steam vent over the funnel and decorate with leaves cut from the pastry trimmings. Brush with milk and bake in a moderate oven (180°C, 350°F, Gas Mark 4) for about 1½ hours. Cover the pastry if necessary after 1 hour to prevent over-browning. *Makes 4–6 servings.*

Devonshire Squab Pie This variation used to include cinnamon, prunes and a little sugar which made it very rich indeed. It was even served with clotted cream for grand occasions.

Leeky Frizzle

The popular name, even shown on restaurant menus, is 'Likky Frizzle'. Leeks are as widely grown in the West Country as in Wales.

1.5 kg/3 lb breast of lamb
600 ml/1 pint beef stock
450 g/1 lb leeks
salt and pepper
675 g/1½ lb mashed potato

Divide the breast into single bones and trim off some of the fat. Place in a saucepan with the stock, bring to the boil, cover and cook gently for about 30 minutes, until tender. Meanwhile, trim and slice the leeks, then cook in a pan of boiling salted water for 10 minutes. Drain the lamb and the leeks.

Season the potato and use to line a greased shallow ovenproof dish. Spoon over the leeks and arrange the lamb on top. Sprinkle with salt and pepper and bake in a hot oven (220°C, 425°F, Gas Mark 7) for 30 minutes, until the lamb is brown and crisp. *Makes 4–6 servings.*

Wiltshire Porkies

450 g/1 lb pork sausagemeat
deep fat or oil to fry
2 medium cooking apples, peeled
4 large sprigs of parsley
Batter
100 g/4 oz plain flour
pinch of salt
1 egg, beaten
300 ml/½ pint milk

First prepare the batter. Sift the flour and salt into a bowl, make a well in the centre and add the egg and milk. Beat well until the batter is smooth.

Divide the sausagemeat into eight equal portions and shape each into a ball. Dip in the batter and deep fry in hot fat or oil for about 7 minutes, until golden brown all over. Drain well, place in a heated serving dish and keep hot. Meanwhile, core and slice the apples. Dip the apple slices and the parsley sprigs in batter and deep fry in the same way until golden brown. Drain well, arrange round the porkies and serve very hot. *Makes 4 servings.*

Pork with Apples and Sage

25 g/1 oz butter
4 pork chops, trimmed
½ teaspoon dried sage
salt and pepper
4 dessert apples, peeled
300 ml/½ pint sweet cider
675 g/1½ lb potatoes, sliced

Melt the butter, add the chops and brown them on both sides. Sprinkle with the sage and salt and pepper. Core and slice the apples, add to the pan and pour over the cider. Bring to the boil, cover and simmer for about 30 minutes, until the chops are tender. Meanwhile, cook the potato in boiling salted water until soft. Drain well, then mash until smooth. Strain the pan juices from cooking the pork and stir into the mashed potato. Place in a hot serving dish and top with the chops and apples. *Makes 4 servings. Illustrated overleaf.*

Jellied Pork Brawn

½ pig's head
1 bouquet garni
6 peppercorns
1 large onion, quartered
1 large carrot, sliced
100 g/4 oz turnip, diced
salt and pepper
¼ teaspoon freshly grated nutmeg

Scrub the head and place in a pan with the bouquet garni, peppercorns, onion, carrot and turnip. Add water to cover and bring slowly to the boil. Skim and boil gently for about 3 hours, until the meat is really tender. Remove from the pan, take the meat from the bones and chop neatly. Skin the tongue and slice thinly. Remove the brains and tie in a piece of muslin. Skim any fat from the surface of the cooking liquid, add the brains and boil until the liquid is reduced by half. Season the chopped and sliced meat with salt, pepper and nutmeg and place in one large or two smaller basins. Strain over the reduced liquid to cover the meat and stand in a cool place until firmly set. Turn out to serve and garnish with parsley. *Makes 6–8 servings. Illustrated overleaf.*

Cornish Pasties

The pasty was an ideal meal for the Cornish tin miners to take down the mine with them, and also for the fishermen to take out in their boats. It was customary for the cook to mark on the pastry the initial of the person for whom it was intended. Those of the crew who disliked onion were given pasties without any and the skipper always had the pasty with most meat in it. It was usual to begin eating from the unmarked end so that if the fish started to bite you could return to your own pasty after the catch had been hauled in.

450 g/1 lb shortcrust pastry
(made with 450 g/1 lb flour, etc.)
350 g/12 oz potato
225 g/8 oz swede
350 g/12 oz onion
450 g/1 lb beef skirt
salt and pepper
beaten egg to brush

Roll out the pastry and cut into six rounds about 15 cm/6 inches in diameter. Cut the potato and swede into small dice and mix with the finely chopped onion and meat. Season well with salt and pepper. Divide the filling between the pastry rounds, brush the edges with beaten egg and bring up opposite sides to meet over the filling. Seal well together and flute the edges. Brush with beaten egg, cut a small steam vent in the top, place on a baking tray and bake in a moderate oven (180°C, 350°F, Gas Mark 4) for about 50 minutes, until the pasties are golden brown. *Makes 6. Illustrated overleaf.*

Tiddy Oggy

This is another pasty, filled with potato, which the Cornish tin miners took with them to eat during their meal break. It fitted conveniently into a trouser pocket and there was no danger of it being crushed because it was harder than the tin they were digging out. In fact, it was said you could drop a good one down the mine shaft without damaging it!

Exeter Stew with Parsley Dumplings

675 g/1½ lb stewing steak, cubed
50 g/2 oz seasoned flour
50 g/2 oz dripping
2 large onions, sliced
2 large carrots, sliced
900 ml/1½ pints beef stock
1 teaspoon vinegar
salt and pepper
Dumplings
100 g/4 oz plain flour
¼ teaspoon baking powder
1 teaspoon salt
½ teaspoon pepper
½ teaspoon dried mixed herbs
2 tablespoons chopped parsley
40 g/1½ oz shredded suet
milk to mix

Above
Cornish Pasties

Right
As well as ways with the plentiful supply of fish, West Country cooks turn their hands to some excellent meat dishes, as shown here: Jellied Pork Brawn (left), Exeter Stew with Parsley Dumplings (centre) and Pork with Apples and Sage (right).

Coat the beef in seasoned flour. Heat the dripping in a large saucepan and use to brown the meat all over. Remove from the pan. Add the onion and carrot to the fat remaining in the pan and fry gently until the onion begins to soften. Stir in the remaining seasoned flour and cook until golden brown. Gradually add the stock and bring to the boil, stirring constantly. Return the meat to the pan with the vinegar and seasoning, bring back to the boil, cover and simmer for 1½ hours.

Meanwhile, make the dumplings. Sift the flour, baking powder, salt and pepper into a bowl and stir in the herbs and suet. Add sufficient milk to make a stiff dough. Divide into 12 portions and shape each into a ball. Place on top of the stew and boil gently for a further 30 minutes. Adjust the seasoning before serving. *Makes 6 servings. Illustrated right.*

Clotted Cream

The counties of Devon and Cornwall are famous for this speciality well beyond their boundaries. The old Cornish name was clouted cream, and a teatime treat, 'Thunder and Lightning', consisted of a Cornish split topped with cream and black treacle.

Clotted cream seems to creep into a great many West Country recipes since using it was never considered an extravagance; there was always some in the larder. Even an everyday pie made with lamb and chopped parsley (affectionately known as lammy pie) always had a layer of clotted cream under the pastry. A bowl of cream was traditionally kept on a cold marble shelf, covered with a white crochet mat weighted with glass beads round the edge.

No Devon or Cornish housewife would stint the cream. It was not only piled up in scones and splits, spread thickly on unbuttered bread with jam and spooned on to fruit pies – but used with imagination in many interesting recipes, including some for sour clotted cream.

Clotting Cream

Take very fresh milk, warm from the cow if possible, and strain it into a large shallow pan. A well-scrubbed copper preserving pan can be used. Leave undisturbed in a cool place for at least 12 hours, or longer if the weather is cold. When all the cream has risen to the surface, transfer the pan gently to the stove, taking great care not to break up the cream. Place over a very low heat for about 30 minutes, or until the top is crusted. Never allow it to boil as the secret of success is to bring the milk just to scalding point. Remove the pan, again using great care, to a cool place, or merely switch off the heat under the pan. It will take about 12 hours for the cream to clot, and it can then be skimmed off with a slotted draining spoon or slice. Any tiny 'clotties' can be strained off by pouring the creamy wade (skimmed milk) through a sieve lined with muslin. This rich milk is good with breakfast cereals or makes what children call 'speckly' tea. *Illustrated overleaf.*

Exmouth Onion Pie

350 g/12 oz shortcrust pastry
(made with 350 g/12 oz flour, etc.)
100 g/4 oz clotted cream
350 g/12 oz onion, chopped
pinch of freshly grated nutmeg
salt and pepper
beaten egg to brush

Roll out the pastry and use just over half to line a 20-cm/8-inch sandwich tin. Combine the cream and onion and season well with the nutmeg, salt and pepper. Turn into the prepared flan case. Use the remaining pastry to make a lid. Brush the edges with beaten egg and seal well together. Prick with a fork and decorate with pastry trimmings. Brush with beaten egg and bake in a moderate oven (180°C, 350°F, Gas Mark 4) for 1 hour, until golden. *Makes 4 servings.*

Sunday-Best Ginger Biscuits

2 eggs, beaten
100 g/4 oz clotted cream
75 g/3 oz castor sugar
1 teaspoon ground ginger
about 450 g/1 lb plain flour

Beat the eggs into the cream. Add the sugar and spice and gradually work in the flour until the mixture forms a smooth dough. Roll out thinly on a lightly floured surface and cut into rounds with a 6-cm/2½-inch fluted biscuit cutter. Arrange on an ungreased baking tray and prick with a fork. Bake in a moderate oven (180°C, 350°F, Gas Mark 4) for about 15 minutes, until pale golden. *Makes about 48.*

Granny Dart's Junket

When Granny made her Sunday junket, little people were warned not to touch the bowl, for fear of making the junket 'cry' or separate.

1.15 litres/2 pints milk
1 tablespoon brandy
2 tablespoons castor sugar
4 teaspoons essence of rennet
freshly grated nutmeg

Warm the milk just to blood heat then remove from the heat and stir in the brandy and sugar. Pour into a glass dish and stir in the rennet. Allow to stand undisturbed until set. Dust the top lightly with grated nutmeg and serve with a bowl of thick clotted cream. *Makes 6–8 servings.*

Rose Cream This elegant kind of junket is made in the same way, using single cream instead of milk, and rose water instead of brandy. It is served with double cream whipped with more rose water and castor sugar to sweeten, and topped with a few pink or red rose petals. *Illustrated overleaf.*

Burnt Cream Pudding

2 eggs
40 g/1½ oz sugar
300 ml/½ pint single cream
100 g/4 oz clotted cream
25 g/1 oz castor sugar

Whisk the eggs with the sugar. Scald the cream, pour into the egg mixture and whisk thoroughly. Transfer to a double saucepan and stir over boiling water until the custard thickens enough to coat the back of the spoon. Remove from the heat and allow to set. Stir the clotted cream to thin it slightly. Spoon alternate layers of custard and cream into four flameproof dishes. Sprinkle the tops with castor sugar and place under a hot grill until the sugar melts and turns golden brown. *Makes 4 servings. Illustrated overleaf.*

Sour Cream Cakes

450 g/1 lb self-raising flour
225 g/8 oz sour clotted cream
100 g/4 oz castor sugar
1 egg, beaten
milk to mix
crushed sugar lumps to sprinkle

Sift the flour and rub in the cream until the mixture is like breadcrumbs. Stir in the sugar. Add the egg and sufficient milk to make a dough which is firm but not stiff. Roll out on a lightly floured surface to a thickness of about 1 cm/½ inch. Stamp into rounds with a 7.5-cm/3-inch biscuit cutter. Place on greased baking trays, brush with milk and sprinkle with a little sugar. Bake in a hot oven (220°C, 425°F, Gas Mark 7) for about 10 minutes until pale golden. *Makes about 24.*

Floury Milk

Farm workers who went out before first light often made a hasty breakfast of this concoction. Also called Gerty Milk, it was really a thin white sauce made of flour and milk, sprinkled with a little sugar, a few currants and a pinch of cinnamon. Sometimes it was eaten like gruel, and sometimes poured over pieces of white bread. A busy farmer's wife often gave each bowl in turn a stir with the same cinnamon stick, when she was in a hurry.

Splits or Chudleighs

450 g/1 lb plain flour
½ teaspoon salt
3 tablespoons milk
250 ml/8 fl oz water
15 g/½ oz fresh yeast
1 teaspoon castor sugar
25 g/1 oz butter, melted

Sift the flour and salt into a bowl. Heat the milk and water together until just warm. Cream the yeast with the sugar and gradually blend in the milk liquid. Make a well in the centre of the dry ingredients and pour in the yeast liquid and melted butter. Mix to a dough, turn out on a floured surface and knead for 5 minutes. Return to the bowl, cover and allow to rise in a warm place for about 1 hour, until double in size. Divide the dough into 12 portions, knead each lightly and shape into a round. Arrange evenly on a greased baking tray, cover and leave in a warm place until the splits are just touching each other. Bake in a hot oven (220°C, 425°F, Gas Mark 7) for about 15 minutes, until well risen and golden. When cooked, the splits will sound hollow when tapped on the base with the knuckles. Place on a wire rack and cover with a clean tea-cloth to keep the crust soft. Split and serve with clotted cream and strawberry jam or treacle. *Makes 12. Illustrated overleaf.*

THE WEST COUNTRY

Clotted cream, the pride of the West, is the result of their enormous yield of rich milk, brimming with thick yellow cream. The West Country housewife does not stint on clotted cream, which is added with a lavish hand to both sweet and savoury dishes. From left: Splits, Rose Cream and Burnt Cream Pudding. Also shown is an old-fashioned butter churner and a selection of butter pats.

The Apple Orchard

Apples are at the heart of many a West Country recipe and provide the famous drink of the region – cider, which is made from fermented apple juice. Cider used to be part of a farm labourer's wages at harvest time and there are many fascinating old country customs connected with apples.

On large farms where all the men and 'maids' gathered for the feast, only the men would go out to the orchard; the women would remain in the house while they secretly roasted some sort of animal or bird, barring the doors so that in spite of the cold, the men would have to wait outside until they could guess what was cooking. It might have been a rabbit, or a rook, or something more bizarre. The custom is still well remembered.

Later in the year when the apples had ripened and almost all had been picked, the small ones were left on the trees for the piskies (pixies).

On Twelfth Night, a farmer's children still all dip pieces of toast into a hot cider cup, solemnly place their 'toasts' in the lowest fork of the oldest tree in the orchard and then all dance round it for luck. These customs of wassailing the trees are far older than any Christian celebration.

Making Cider

'Scrumpy' or rough homemade cider is a potent brew, but when fully matured it can have many of the qualities of a fine wine; very dry and still, or sweeter and sparkling. Draught cider may taste innocent enough but it is highly alcoholic and needs a strong head if consumed in any quantity. The old country method used nothing but pure juice from tart firm apples which were left out of doors for a while, spread out on racks in the sun. The apples were then chopped and crushed in a wooden press (metal must never come into contact with cider), though sometimes an old stone sink was used instead of a wooden barrel. The juice was then extracted from the crushed apple pulp. The favourite way of doing this was to put the pulp in a clean pillow-case and run it through an old-fashioned mangle with wooden rollers. After fermenting, sugar was added only if a sweet cider was required. Many farmers make their own scrumpy today in much the same way. Cider takes about three months to mature but should really be used up before it is nine months old.

Mulled Cider Cup

When the next crop of apples is ready, cider from the previous pressing is often used up to serve at the harvest festival in a mulled punch.

The cider is slowly heated with extra sugar if required, sliced oranges and apples, and spices such as cloves, nutmeg and cinnamon added to taste. In the days of the old smugglers and their illicit kegs of brandy, a few tablespoons of brandy were often slipped in to improve the flavour. *Illustrated overleaf.*

Orchard Sweets

Apples are mentioned as ingredients for cookery in manuscripts dating from medieval times, so it is not surprising that there are traditional apple recipes in almost every part of the country. Pears as well were among the first fruit trees grown in England. In a countryside dotted with orchards, where cider is the favourite drink, there are many old recipes for apple puddings and cakes.

Apple 'In and Out'

450 g/1 lb self-raising flour
pinch of salt
225 g/8 oz shredded suet
100 g/4 oz sugar
675 g/1½ lb cooking apples

Sift the flour and salt into a basin and stir in the suet and sugar. Peel, core and chop the apples and stir into the dry ingredients with sufficient cold water to make a soft dough. When evenly combined, turn into a greased 1.5-litre/2½-pint pudding basin. Cover and steam or boil for 2½ hours. Turn out and serve with a syrup sauce. *Makes 4 servings.*

Apple Dappy

175 g/6 oz plain flour
75 g/3 oz lard
milk to mix
450 g/1 lb cooking apples
100 g/4 oz castor sugar
7 tablespoons water
1 tablespoon golden syrup
25 g/1 oz butter

Sift the flour into a bowl and rub in the lard. Add sufficient milk to make a stiff dough. Roll out thinly on a floured surface into an oblong shape. Peel, core and chop the apples, scatter over the pastry and sprinkle with the sugar. Roll up from the long side like a Swiss roll and cut into 2.5-cm/1-inch slices. Arrange these slices close together in a roasting tin, cut sides uppermost. Place the water, syrup and butter in a saucepan and heat until the butter melts. Stir, then drizzle this mixture over the apple dappies. Bake in a moderate oven (180°C, 350°F, Gas Mark 4) for about 30 minutes, until golden brown on top. Serve hot with cream. *Makes 4 servings.*

Dorset Apple Cake

350 g/12 oz cooking apples, peeled
100 g/4 oz plain flour
¼ teaspoon baking powder
pinch of salt
50 g/2 oz butter
50 g/2 oz castor sugar
1 egg, beaten
3 sugar lumps, crushed

Core and chop the apples. Sift the flour with the baking powder and salt. Cream the butter and castor sugar until light and fluffy then gradually beat in the egg. Fold in the chopped apple and the flour mixture. Turn into a greased 20-cm/8-inch sandwich tin and sprinkle the crushed sugar lumps over the top. Bake in a moderately hot oven (200°C, 400°F, Gas Mark 6) for about 30 minutes, until firm to the touch and golden brown on top. Serve warm with clotted cream. *Makes 4–6 servings. Illustrated overleaf.*

Buttered Pears

150 ml/¼ pint strong still cider
½ teaspoon freshly grated nutmeg
50 g/2 oz soft brown sugar
25 g/1 oz butter
4 firm dessert pears, peeled

Place the cider in a saucepan with the nutmeg, sugar and butter and heat until the sugar has dissolved and the butter melted. Halve and core the pears and place in a shallow ovenproof dish with the rounded sides uppermost. Pour the cider liquid over the pears, cover and cook in a moderate oven (160°C, 325°F, Gas Mark 3) for about 40 minutes, or until the pears are just soft. A few sultanas or seedless raisins can also be scattered over the pears before cooking. *Makes 4 servings.*

Cheddar Cheese

So well-known is this golden-yellow hard cheese that it is often referred to merely as Cheddar, and a cheese of this type is made in many other countries far from Cheddar Gorge, the district of its origin. Some Cheddars are so pale as to be more creamy than yellow, but the true product of Somerset and Devon is the colour of a harvest moon. By contrast, a delicious farmhouse cheese of the region, called Blue Vinny, is a rarity not easy to come by these days, even locally, but it would be well worth a long search to find it.

Bath Oliver Biscuits

The secret of this recipe has been well guarded by the manufacturers since the time when the biscuits were first prepared for the wealthy and decidedly overweight patients of a well-known Dr. Oliver of that town. Some cooks claim to know what went into the original biscuits and that the delicious nutty flavour comes from the use of malt. No marriage could be happier than that between Bath Oliver biscuits and Cheddar cheese.

Overleaf
Cider is to the West Country as wine is to France. Fermenting cider apples become in time scrumpy, or even Mulled Cider Cup, while other varieties are held back to make delicious recipes like Dorset Apple Cake, shown in the picture.

Cakes, Buns and Biscuits

Yeasted mixtures are extremely popular in the West Country where oven baking is much preferred to the simple girdle or griddle method of cooking. Most bakers bake tuff cakes, trays of delicate soft bread rolls, all sticking together like golden brown cobblestones which have to be pulled apart to be eaten.

Sally Lunn Cakes

The history of these round buns with golden tops and white bases goes much further back in time than the popular explanation that they were sold in the streets of Bath by a certain Sally Lunn. The old street cry in Norman French 'Soleil et Lune' describes them exactly – like the sun on one side, the moon on the other.

300 ml/½ pint milk
25 g/1 oz butter
15 g/½ oz fresh yeast
2 teaspoons castor sugar
2 eggs
450 g/1 lb plain flour
¾ teaspoon salt
150 ml/¼ pint double cream
castor sugar to sprinkle

Warm two 12.5-cm/5-inch or 15-cm/6-inch cake tins and grease them. Place the milk and butter in a saucepan and heat gently until the butter has melted. Cool until lukewarm. Cream the yeast with half the sugar and gradually blend in the milk mixture, then beat in 1 egg.

Sift the flour and salt into a bowl, make a well in the centre and add the yeast liquid. Mix to a soft dough, cover and leave in a warm place until double in size. Turn out and knead for 3 minutes. Divide the dough in half and shape each portion to fit a warmed cake tin. Cover and allow to stand until double in size. Uncover and bake in a hot oven (220°C, 425°F, Gas Mark 7) for 15 minutes. Meanwhile, separate the second egg and beat the yolk. Use to brush the tops of the cakes, return them to the oven and bake for a further 5–10 minutes, until golden brown. Cool slightly on a wire rack. Whip the cream with the rest of the sugar. Whisk the remaining egg white until stiff and fold into the sweetened cream. When the cakes are still slightly warm, split each into three layers, fill with the sweetened cream, reshape and sprinkle the tops with sugar. *Makes 2.*

Revel Buns

In the West Country, annual Revels are held similar to the Wakes of the North, the great Goose Fairs of the Shires, the Hiring Fairs of East Anglia and the rest. Every such occasion has its special delicacy, named for the occasion, and it is typical of the West Country that their Revel Buns are made with saffron and clotted cream.

generous pinch of saffron strands
150 ml/¼ pint hot milk
450 g/1 lb plain flour
¼ teaspoon salt
½ teaspoon ground cinnamon
100 g/4 oz butter
100 g/4 oz currants
20 g/¾ oz fresh yeast
1 teaspoon castor sugar
100 g/4 oz clotted cream
2 eggs, beaten
icing sugar to sprinkle

Snip the saffron strands, stir into the hot milk and allow to stand for 30 minutes, then strain. Sift the flour, salt and cinnamon into a bowl and rub in the butter. Stir in the currants and make a well in the centre. Cream the yeast with the sugar and gradually blend in the saffron milk, cream and most of the beaten eggs. Pour into the dry ingredients and mix to a soft dough. Turn out on a floured surface and knead for 3 minutes. Return to the bowl, cover and allow to stand in a cold place or in the refrigerator to rise slowly for 8 hours, until double in size. Divide into 16 pieces and shape each into a round bun. Arrange on greased baking trays, cover and allow to prove in a warm place for about 20 minutes. Brush with the remaining beaten egg and bake in a moderately hot oven (190°C, 375°F, Gas Mark 5) for about 15 minutes, until firm and golden brown. Cool on a wire rack and sprinkle with sifted icing sugar. *Makes 16.*

Saffron Dough Cake

generous pinch of saffron strands
300 ml/½ pint hot milk
15 g/½ oz fresh yeast
75 g/3 oz castor sugar
450 g/1 lb plain flour
175 g/6 oz butter
175 g/6 oz currants
50 g/2 oz chopped mixed peel

Infuse the saffron in the hot milk for 2 hours then strain and heat the liquid to lukewarm. Cream the yeast with 1 teaspoon sugar and gradually blend in the flavoured milk. Reserve 1 teaspoon of flour. Sift the remainder into a bowl, rub in the butter, make a well in the centre and pour in the yeast liquid. Sprinkle the reserved flour over the surface of the yeast liquid and allow to stand in a warm place for about 15 minutes, until frothy. Add the fruit and peel and remaining sugar and mix to a soft dough. Cover and allow to rise in a warm place until double in size. Turn out on a floured surface, knead lightly and shape to fit a greased 20-cm/8-inch cake tin. Bake in a moderate oven (180°C, 350°F, Gas Mark 4) for about 1 hour, until firm to the touch and golden brown on top. Leave to cool in the tin. Serve fresh in slices with clotted cream.

If the dough cake is not freshly baked, slices can be toasted and spread with butter.

Figgy Hobbin

In the West Country 'figgy' means full of raisins or currants rather than figs. Currany Obbin is an oven-baked currant pastry, the oven often being called ob'n or obbin by Cornish folk.

225 g/8 oz shortcrust pastry
(made with 225 g/8 oz flour, etc.)
100–175 g/4–6 oz seedless raisins or currants
25 g/1 oz sugar
beaten egg to brush

Roll out the pastry thinly to a rectangle about 25 × 20 cm/10 × 8 inches. Sprinkle with the fruit and sugar, keeping a border of 1 cm/½ inch clear all round. Brush the edges with beaten egg and roll up from the long edge to make a roll. Place on a greased baking tray with the seal underneath and brush with beaten egg. Prick the top with a fork and bake in a moderately hot oven (200°C, 400°F, Gas Mark 6) for about 40 minutes, until golden brown all over. Serve cut into slices. *Makes 4–6 servings.*

Cornish Fairings

These are small biscuits with a crunchy texture sold at local markets and fairs.

100 g/4 oz plain flour
pinch of salt
1 teaspoon baking powder
1 teaspoon bicarbonate of soda
1 teaspoon ground ginger
¼ teaspoon ground cinnamon
¼ teaspoon ground mixed spice
50 g/2 oz butter
50 g/2 oz castor sugar
3 tablespoons golden syrup, warmed

Sift the flour with the salt, baking powder, bicarbonate of soda and spices into a bowl. Rub in the butter and stir in the sugar. Add the warmed syrup and mix well. Shape the dough into small balls and place well apart on greased baking trays. Bake in a moderately hot oven (190°C, 375°F, Gas Mark 5) for 15–20 minutes. Leave on the trays for 5 minutes, then cool on a wire rack. *Makes about 25.*

Easter Biscuits

These bright yellow biscuits are a traditional treat for Easter Sunday, so much enjoyed that, after Church in the morning, children would run about eating them for the rest of the day.

175 g/6 oz plain flour
50 g/2 oz rice flour
1 teaspoon ground mixed spice
100 g/4 oz butter
100 g/4 oz castor sugar
2 egg yolks
75 g/3 oz currants
1–2 tablespoons brandy or milk

Sift the flours with the spice. Cream the butter and sugar together until light and fluffy. Beat in the egg yolks, one at a time, then add the fruit. Work in the flour mixture with enough brandy or milk to make a stiff paste. Turn out on a floured surface and knead until smooth. Roll out to a thickness of about 1 cm/½ inch and cut into 7.5-cm/3-inch rounds with a fluted biscuit cutter.

Place the biscuits on greased baking trays and bake in a moderate oven (180°C, 350°F, Gas Mark 4) for 15–20 minutes, until pale golden. Leave on the trays for 5 minutes then cool on a wire rack. *Makes about 25.*

East Anglia

The peculiar magic of this region lies in its seemingly remote and secret character. Although it is really much closer to London than the West Country, somehow it is far less well known to Londoners and seems farther away. It is a place of flat sea marshes, sand dunes and deserted shingle beaches along the coast, and winding waterways inland. Some people find a certain kinship there with the Dutch landscape, especially in spring when the Lincolnshire bulb fields are in bloom. In Lincolnshire, too, there is another speciality; samphire which grows near the sea, a succulent plant almost like seaweed, yet which tastes more like asparagus when cooked as a vegetable, and makes an interesting pickle.

Wild fowl abound in the Fens and it is probably the only part of Britain where wild duck is still frequently on the menu.

Vegetables are the principal harvest rather than grain, and Lincoln grown peas and beans for canning and freezing are world renowned. Sugar beet grows there too, and an unusual variety of the same family, spinach beet. In country markets the white ribs and stems of spinach beet are sold tied in bundles, each with a sprig of mint, to be cooked like asparagus. The leaves are cooked separately and eaten like spinach.

East Anglia has a number of big coastal towns, including Harwich and the fishing ports of Great Yarmouth and Lowestoft. The latter are famous for their herrings and bloaters. A bloater for tea was a Victorian delicacy in many London homes yet cheap enough to be enjoyed by any Cockney. Even today, bloaters are relatively cheap considering their fine flavour. The oyster beds of Colchester provide a costlier feast (as popular in summer as the whitebait feasts of Greenwich) and have done since the days when Roman invaders used to send them home carefully packed alive in tanks. The shells of a particularly choice variety from the mouth of the River Colne can still be found on sites in ancient Rome itself.

The unmistakable flat terrain of East Anglia looks up to a wide sky of limitless horizons.

Suffolk Spinach Soup

450 g/1 lb spinach
1 small turnip
2 medium onions
2 medium carrots
2 sticks celery
50 g/2 oz butter
1 teaspoon chopped parsley
pinch of dried thyme
1.15 litres/2 pints beef stock
salt and pepper
Dumplings
100 g/4 oz self-raising flour
pinch of salt
50 g/2 oz shredded suet

Wash the spinach well and shred finely. Finely chop the other vegetables. Melt the butter in a large saucepan, add all the vegetables and stir over gentle heat for about 5 minutes. Add the herbs and stock, season with salt and pepper and cook for 20 minutes, until the vegetables are soft. Sieve or liquidise in a blender and return to the rinsed-out pan with 600 ml/1 pint water. Bring back to the boil, then allow to simmer.

Sift the flour and salt into a bowl, stir in the suet and sufficient cold water to make a stiff dough. Divide into small pieces and roll into tiny dumplings. Add to the soup and boil gently for 15 minutes. Serve very hot. *Makes 6–8 servings.*

Yarmouth Fish Soup

1 kg/2 lb cod or other white fish
2 medium onions, quartered
1 stick of celery, sliced
2 tablespoons tomato purée
150 ml/¼ pint white wine
2 tablespoons flour
150 ml/¼ pint milk
1 teaspoon chopped fennel
finely grated rind of 1 lemon
2 tablespoons chopped parsley
salt and pepper

Put the fish, onion and celery into a saucepan and add 1.5 litres/2¾ pints cold water. Bring to the boil and simmer for 15 minutes, or until the fish is just cooked. Take the fish from the pan, remove the skin and bones and return these to the vegetables and stock. Continue simmering for a further 30 minutes. Strain and return the stock to the pan with the tomato purée and wine. Cut the fish into chunks and add to the pan. Blend the flour with the milk, taking care that there are no lumps. Stir in a little of the hot liquid, blend well and add to the soup. Bring to the boil, stirring constantly. Add the fennel, lemon rind and parsley. Season well before serving. *Makes 6–8 servings. Illustrated overleaf.*

Bloaters

This variety of cured herring comes from the Norfolk coast where, in the late Nineteenth Century, the large catch was handled by girls who travelled south from Northumberland and even East Scotland. The herring is left unsplit, lightly salted and smoked without removing the gut. This gives the fish a gamy flavour and, if not freshly cured, they are rank and unpalatable. Bloaters may be grilled or baked, split to put a knob of butter in each, then reshaped for serving with bread and butter or toast. Bloater paste can be made by skinning and boning baked bloaters then mashing the flesh with an equal weight of butter and a little seasoning.

Cockles and Whelks

These are also caught off the Norfolk coast, and used to be eaten very freshly boiled with bread and butter and a sauceboat of melted butter.

An Eighteenth Century recipe for roast mutton recommends that freshly cooked cockles be placed in incisions made all over the surface before roasting and serving with horseradish.

Lowestoft Herrings and Mustard Sauce

Sea water is always used to cook herrings in Lowestoft and is said to make the flesh firm and just sufficiently flavoured without being over salty.

fresh sea water or well-salted fresh water
8 large herrings, cleaned
Sauce
25 g/1 oz butter
15 g/½ oz flour
300 ml/½ pint milk
1 teaspoon dry mustard
little wine vinegar
1 tablespoon sugar

Bring a pan of sea or salted water to the boil, add the herrings and boil rapidly for 6–8 minutes. Meanwhile, melt the butter in a clean saucepan, stir in the flour and cook for 1 minute. Gradually add the milk and bring to the boil, stirring constantly, until the sauce thickens. Mix the mustard with sufficient wine vinegar to make a thin cream. Stir into the sauce with the sugar. Serve with the freshly boiled and drained herrings. *Makes 8 servings.*

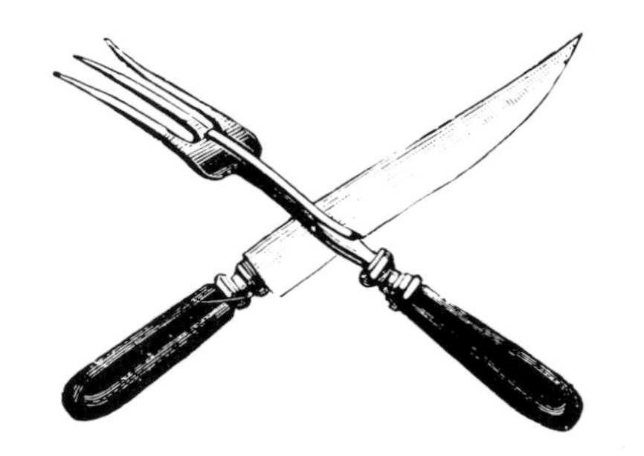

Lincolnshire Stuffed Chine

A speciality traditionally eaten on May Day, but now frequently available in Lincolnshire butchers' shops, it is vividly striped in green and pink; best eaten cold with vinegar.

1 (1.5-kg/3-lb) neck chine
or collar of bacon
1 large bunch of parsley
12 sprigs of thyme
12 sprigs of marjoram
1 lettuce heart
6 spring onions
few young raspberry leaves
few young blackcurrant leaves

Soak the bacon joint in cold water for 24 hours. Drain, dry and score it deeply down to the bone. Wash and dry the herbs, lettuce, onions and leaves and chop them all finely. Insert this mixture into the deep cuts, packing it in tightly. Cover the chine with greaseproof paper or foil, place in a roasting tin and cook in a moderate oven (180°C, 350°F, Gas Mark 4), allowing 20 minutes per 450 g/1 lb, plus an extra 20 minutes.

Remove the joint from the wrapping and cool on a rack over a dish, allowing surplus liquid to drain away. Serve cold. *Makes 8 servings.*

Aslett

450 g/1 lb pig's liver
450 g/1 lb pig's lights
225 g/8 oz onions
12 sage leaves
450 g/1 lb sausagemeat
225 g/8 oz fine fresh white breadcrumbs
salt and pepper
2 teaspoons ground mace
2 teaspoons freshly grated nutmeg
pig's caul, veil or flead
(available from the butcher)

Put the liver, lights and onions into a saucepan with sufficient water almost to cover. Bring to the boil and simmer until very tender. Remove the meat and onions and mince finely. Chop the sage leaves, add to the minced meat with the sausagemeat, breadcrumbs, seasoning and spices. Knead well and shape into a long roll. Cover with the caul, tuck the ends underneath and place in a greased shallow ovenproof dish. Bake in a moderate oven (160°C, 325°F, Gas Mark 3) for 2 hours, when the outside should be nice and crisp. Leave to cool in the dish. Serve cut into thick slices. *Makes about 10 servings.*

Pork Cheese

A savoury mould which is sometimes made with the pig's head and called head cheese, makes use of very cheap cuts of meat. In some districts the pig's feet are called pettitoes.

pig's feet, hock or knuckle
(or a combination of these)
sage leaves
salt and pepper

Place the meat in a pan with a few chopped sage leaves. Cover with water and bring to the boil. Simmer for at least 2 hours, until the meat drops from the bone. Remove from the pan, discard all the bones and shred the meat as finely as possible. Return to the pan containing the stock. Season well and add a little extra chopped sage if desired. Simmer for 15 minutes and turn into moulds, distributing the meat and liquid equally. Leave to become quite cold and set. Turn out to serve.

Minced Ham Loaf or Pie

350 g/12 oz plain flour
pinch of salt
175 g/6 oz lard
milk to brush
Filling
575 g/1¼ lb ham trimmings
1 medium onion
salt and pepper
2 eggs

Sift the flour and salt into a bowl and rub in the lard. Add sufficient water (about 4 tablespoons) to make a stiff dough. Roll out two-thirds of the pastry and use to line a greased 0.5-kg/1-lb loaf tin. Mince the ham and onion. Season and turn into the tin. Spread out the mixture then make two hollows using the back of a spoon. Into each hollow break a raw egg. Roll out the remaining pastry to make a lid, dampen and seal the edges. Decorate with pastry trimmings. Brush with milk and bake in a moderate oven (180°C, 350°F, Gas Mark 4) for 1–1½ hours, until golden brown. Serve hot or cold. *Makes 4 servings. Illustrated right.*

Roast Wild Duck

Birds such as mallards abound on the Norfolk Broads. Locally they are served very underdone.

1 wild duck
50 g/2 oz butter
juice of 2 oranges
2 teaspoons flour
juice of ½ lemon
2 teaspoons sugar
pinch of salt
pinch of cayenne pepper
2 tablespoons port
1 tablespoon mushroom ketchup

Stuff the bird with the butter. Put into a roasting tin with the orange juice. Roast in a hot oven (220°C, 425°F, Gas Mark 7) for 20–25 minutes, basting occasionally with the juice. To serve well done, increase cooking time to 40–45 minutes. Sprinkle with the flour and baste again. Add the remaining ingredients to the juices in the pan. Heat through, stirring, and serve as a sauce. *Makes 2–3 servings. Illustrated right.*

Right
Cooking on the range . . . and what could be more welcoming than this food from the Fens. From left: Yarmouth Fish Soup, Minced Ham Loaves and Roast Wild Duck, while the orange sauce for the duck is keeping warm on top of the range.

Stewed Breast of Veal with Asparagus

1 (1.25-kg/2½-lb) breast of veal
50 g/2 oz butter or dripping
25 g/1 oz flour
600 ml/1 pint beef stock
1 medium onion stuck with 2 cloves
450 g/1 lb asparagus or sprue
salt and pepper

Cut the veal into pieces about 7.5 cm/3 inches square and trim off excess fat. Melt the butter or dripping in a flameproof casserole. When very hot fry the pieces of veal until golden brown. Sprinkle in the flour and stir for a few minutes. Gradually add the stock and bring to the boil, stirring constantly. Add the onion. Cover and simmer for about 2 hours, until the veal is tender. Cut the asparagus into small pieces, discarding the woody stalks, add to the meat and cook gently for a further 20 minutes. Season to taste before serving. *Makes 4 servings.*
Note When asparagus or sprue are not available peas may be used instead.

Lincolnshire Poacher's Pudding

This succulent rabbit and bacon pudding is probably not exclusive to Lincolnshire, since many a plump young rabbit has found its way into the pot as part of a farm worker's unofficial perks.

350 g/12 oz self-raising flour
pinch of salt
175 g/6 oz shredded suet
Filling
450 g/1 lb rabbit portions
225 g/8 oz lean collar of bacon, soaked overnight
2 medium onions, chopped
2 medium cooking apples, chopped
1 medium carrot, diced
salt and pepper
cider or chicken stock

Sift the flour and salt into a bowl and stir in the suet. Add sufficient cold water to make a firm dough. Knead lightly on a floured surface. Roll out two-thirds of the pastry to line a greased 1.25-litre/2-pint pudding basin.

Place the rabbit portions in a pan, cover with cold water and bring to the boil. Drain well. Cut the bacon into cubes. Fill the lined pudding basin with layers of rabbit, bacon, onion, apple and carrot, seasoning each layer. Pour in cider or chicken stock to almost cover the filling. Roll out the remaining pastry to make a lid, dampen the edges and seal well together. Cover with greased greaseproof paper or foil, with a pleat in the centre, and tie on with string. Place in a saucepan, add boiling water to come halfway up the sides of the basin and boil for 4 hours, adding more boiling water when necessary. Serve the pudding from the basin with a clean napkin folded round the outside. *Makes 4–6 servings.*

Roast Rabbit in Milk

1 young rabbit, cleaned
2 medium onions
50 g/2 oz fresh white breadcrumbs
1 tablespoon chopped sage
or 1 teaspoon dried sage
salt and pepper
25 g/1 oz butter, melted
25 g/1 oz dripping
1 tablespoon flour
600 ml/1 pint milk

Leave the rabbit whole and soak it in salted water for 2 hours. Boil the onions in water until just tender. Chop them and mix with the breadcrumbs, sage, seasoning, and melted butter. Stuff the rabbit with this mixture and sew up the opening to enclose the stuffing. Place the rabbit in a roasting tin, dot with the dripping and sprinkle with flour, salt and pepper. Pour the milk round the rabbit and bake in a moderate oven (160°C, 325°F, Gas Mark 3) for 2 hours, or until tender, basting frequently with the milk. The rabbit should be nicely browned with a delicious gravy. Serve with mashed potatoes and a green vegetable. *Makes 4 servings.*

Pigeon Pie and Figgy Pastry

Rook pie was often made after rook shoots in May when farmers were glad to get rid of some of the birds. Today, rooks have become more scarce and pigeons are often used instead.

8 young pigeon breasts, skinned
100 g/4 oz streaky bacon
1 teaspoon chopped onion
1 teaspoon chopped thyme
salt and pepper
150 ml/¼ pint chicken stock
Pastry
350 g/12 oz self-raising flour
salt and pepper
175 g/6 oz lard or margarine
75 g/3 oz currants
75 g/3 oz seedless raisins

Soak the pigeon breasts overnight in cold water. Drain and pat dry then place in a 1.75-litre/3-pint pie dish. Cut the bacon into 1-cm/½-inch pieces, add to the pigeon with the onion and thyme. Season with salt and pepper and pour in the stock.

Sift the flour with a little salt and pepper into a bowl. Rub in the fat until the mixture resembles fine breadcrumbs. Add the dried fruit and mix with sufficient cold water to make a stiff dough. Turn on to a floured board and roll out thickly to cover the pie dish. Lightly grease a sheet of greaseproof paper or foil, put over the pastry and tie down under the rim of the dish. Place in a large pan and add sufficient boiling water to come halfway up the sides of the dish. Cover with a lid and simmer for 3 hours, adding more boiling water when necessary. Serve with vegetables and gooseberry jelly. *Makes 8 servings.*

Pickled Samphire

Samphire (also known as Peter's Cress or Rock Samphire) grows wild on the shingle and salt marshes around Snettisham in Norfolk. It is at its best in July. Although usually served boiled as a hot vegetable with butter, it is sometimes pickled.

Gather the samphire and soak for about 3 hours in a brine of water and salt, or in sea water. Place in a pan and cover with a mixture of three parts white vinegar to one part water and a little salt. Cover with a lid and simmer for 30 minutes. Leave in the pan until cold, then pack the samphire into pots or jars and cover with the cooking liquid mixed with a little fresh vinegar. It should remain a good green colour.

Suffolk Lemon Solid

2 lemons
600 ml/1 pint milk
175 g/6 oz castor sugar
25 g/1 oz gelatine

Grate the rind from the lemons and add to the milk. Heat gently almost to boiling point. Stir in the sugar until dissolved. Squeeze the juice from the lemons into a small basin. Sprinkle over the gelatine. Place the basin in a pan of hot water and stir until the gelatine has completely dissolved. Add to the lemon milk and stir until the curd separates. Pour all into a rinsed mould and leave to set. Turn out to serve if liked. *Makes 4 servings. Illustrated overleaf.*

Brandy Snaps

These are traditional 'fairings', meant to be eaten by folk while wandering round the market place. If correctly made, they really do snap when broken in half, although today they are often served filled with whipped cream.

75 g/3 oz butter
175 g/6 oz golden syrup
100 g/4 oz castor sugar
100 g/4 oz plain flour
1 teaspoon ground ginger

Melt the butter and syrup together in a saucepan over gentle heat. Stir in the sugar and remove from the heat. Sift the flour and ground ginger and add gradually, mixing well. Put teaspoons of the mixture on to greased baking trays, keeping them about 10 cm/4 inches apart to allow for spreading. Bake in a moderately hot oven (190°C, 375°F, Gas Mark 5) for 10–15 minutes, until light golden brown. Allow to stand for a few seconds then remove with a palette knife and curl round the greased handle of a wooden spoon. If they harden before curling, heat through in the oven for a few moments to soften again. Cool on a wire rack and fill with piped whipped cream if wished. *Makes about 30. Illustrated overleaf.*

Cambridge Syllabub

This recipe, a sweet delight enjoyed in many parts of England under the same name but with various spellings, can be made with wine, sherry or Marsala. It was originally made with sack, a dark sweet sherry. The Cambridge version is particularly delicious and, unlike most syllabubs, has no lemon in it.

Take 300 ml/½ pint sweet white dessert wine, 6 tablespoons brandy and 4 tablespoons castor sugar and stir vigorously together in a large bowl until the sugar dissolves. Gradually whip in 600 ml/1 pint double cream. When the mixture is thick, serve in wine or dessert glasses, delicately sprinkled with grated nutmeg. *Makes 6 servings. Illustrated left.*

Deep-Dish Gooseberry Pie

675 g/1½ lb gooseberries
100 g/4 oz soft brown sugar
50 g/2 oz butter
4 tablespoons water
225 g/8 oz prepared flaky pastry
milk to brush
castor sugar to sprinkle

Top and tail the gooseberries. Place a pie funnel in a deep 1.25-litre/2-pint pie dish, then add the gooseberries, sprinkling each layer with sugar and dotting with the butter. Pour over the water. Moisten the rim of the dish. Roll out the pastry to make a lid then reroll the pastry trimmings. Use to make a strip round the rim of the dish, press on well and brush with water. Cover with the pastry lid and press to seal. Flute the edges, brush with milk and bake in a hot oven (220°C, 425°F, Gas Mark 7) for 20 minutes, then reduce to 200°C, 400°F, Gas Mark 6 for a further 20 minutes. Sprinkle with castor sugar to serve. *Makes 4–6 servings. Illustrated left.*

Left

A punt for two on the River Cam, Champagne on ice and a slim volume of verse . . . then what more elegant fare than Cambridge Syllabub and Brandy Snaps with cream, Suffolk Lemon Solid and Deep Dish Gooseberry Pie?

Frumenty

There is no part of the country except the North of Scotland where this ancient recipe is unknown, sometimes under the name of Furmenty or Furmitty. In East Anglia, it is simply soaked boiled wheat, strained and cooked again in milk with dried fruit, sugar and spices. In other regions, beaten eggs are stirred in to turn it into a kind of custard. It is as much a part of the country pattern of living in mid-Lent on Mothering Sunday as pancakes are on Shrove Tuesday.

Ipswich Almond Pudding

This is a rich pudding made for special occasions and the recipe given here dates from the Eighteenth Century.

50 g/2 oz fresh white breadcrumbs
175 g/6 oz ground almonds
50 g/2 oz castor sugar
450 ml/$\frac{3}{4}$ pint warm milk
150 ml/$\frac{1}{4}$ pint warm double cream
1 teaspoon orange flower or rose water
3 large eggs
25 g/1 oz butter

Steep the breadcrumbs, ground almonds and sugar in the milk and cream for 30 minutes. Mix in the orange flower or rose water. Beat the eggs lightly. Pour the breadcrumb mixture over the beaten eggs and blend thoroughly. Grease a pie dish with a little of the butter and pour in the pudding mixture. Dot with the remaining butter and bake in a moderate oven (180°C, 350°F, Gas Mark 4) for 30 minutes. *Makes 4 servings.*

Norfolk Dumplings

These are made from risen white bread dough (see page 83). Form into small balls, cover with a damp cloth and leave in a warm place until slightly increased in size. Drop into a large pan of simmering salted water. Cook for 6–7 minutes, until the dumplings rise to the surface. Strain and serve with melted butter and demerara sugar or a jam sauce.

Suffolk Buns

These are members of a large family of buns, made from a similar basic recipe to which various ingredients, according to the region, are added.

450 g/1 lb plain flour
15 g/$\frac{1}{2}$ oz baking powder
$\frac{1}{2}$ teaspoon salt
175 g/6 oz butter
75 g/3 oz sultanas
175 g/6 oz castor sugar
1 teaspoon caraway seeds (optional)
2 eggs, beaten
about 3–4 tablespoons milk
beaten egg to brush
castor sugar to sprinkle

Sift the flour, baking powder and salt into a bowl. Rub in the butter until the mixture resembles fine breadcrumbs. Stir in the sultanas, sugar and caraway seeds. Add the eggs and sufficient milk to make a fairly stiff dough. Roll out on a floured surface to a thickness of about 2.5 cm/1 inch and cut into 6-cm/2$\frac{1}{2}$-inch rounds with a biscuit cutter. Place on a greased baking tray, brush with beaten egg and sprinkle with sugar. Bake in a hot oven (220°C, 425°F, Gas Mark 7) for 15–20 minutes. *Makes about 12.*

Rock Buns Add 50 g/2 oz chopped mixed peel and only 50 g/2 oz sultanas to the dry ingredients. Omit the caraway seeds. Instead of rolling out, place tablespoons of the mixture on greased baking trays in rough heaps.

Grantham Gingerbread Cake

An unusual white gingerbread cake, made in Grantham, is strongly flavoured but contains no syrup or treacle to give it colour.

100 g/4 oz butter
100 g/4 oz castor sugar
3 eggs
225 g/8 oz plain flour
25 g/1 oz ground ginger
1 teaspoon baking powder
milk to mix

Cream the butter and sugar until light and fluffy and beat in the eggs one at a time. Sift the flour, ginger and baking powder together and fold into the creamed mixture, adding a little milk if necessary, to make a soft dropping consistency. Spoon into a well greased 0.5-kg/1-lb loaf tin and bake in a moderate oven (160°C, 325°F, Gas Mark 3) for 1¼–1½ hours, until firm to the touch.

Sugar Beer

A traditional harvest drink, this is usually made only at the time of the big farm harvest-home party. Its keeping qualities are very limited, 3–4 days maximum. It is very refreshing and, compared with other beers, quite quickly made.

4.5 litres/8 pints water
300 ml/½ pint hops
honey to sweeten
1 slice toast
1 tablespoon brewers' yeast

Put the water and hops into a large pan. Bring to the boil and simmer for 2 hours. Strain into an earthenware or plastic container and sweeten to taste with honey. Float the toast on top with the yeast sprinkled over it. Cover with a clean cloth and leave overnight. The following day remove the toast and skim off any froth. Keep cool until required. *Makes about 2.25 litres/4 pints.*

London

As befits a capital city, bustling London Town has always been ahead of the rest of the country in welcoming new imported foods and new cooking techniques. The mighty Port of London has, over the centuries, admitted an endless throng of foreign immigrants (each it seems with a favourite recipe or two among the family baggage), ready to settle down and ply a profitable trade within sound of Bow Bells. Since the first returning Crusader caused a sensation with his barrels of rice, sugar and China oranges, foods strange to the British palate have arrived, been accepted, and gradually woven into the glorious tapestry of our national cuisine.

London has always been too large for its own comfort, relying on the pretty villages such as Chelsea, Kensington and Hammersmith, which once stood at a distance, for milk and vegetables, while meat and poultry arrived from the country.

The sheer size of the city has, since medieval times, made it necessary for people of every class to eat away from home. Itinerant street sellers made a good living with their trays of hot pies, tarts and fritters, before Dick Whittington became Lord Mayor of London. Cookshops flourished in the Middle Ages and the wartime British restaurant was the direct descendant of the humble East End Cockney eating house. In better times the more affluent dined at midday in Steak Houses, Chop Houses or Clubs. Every tavern sold food or had a stall outside doing a brisk trade.

The Thames has always been more than a river, being London's most ancient and convenient thoroughfare. But only in the Nineteenth Century did it become polluted. Earlier it teemed with fish, from the long forgotten lamprey to the kingly salmon. Being tidal, it also produced such delicacies as whitebait and sprats.

Londoners have always been sophisticated diners at every level of the social scale compared with country dwellers.

The flavour of London's cooking is unique because it depends more on the taste of its people than the products it can grow or raise.

A familiar skyline seen from the River Thames.

Soups

The Lord Mayor's Banquet often begins with a real turtle soup, but the great London favourite is an imitation named in its honour.

Mock Turtle Soup

This soup may not taste exactly like the real thing but its name undoubtedly comes from the fact that the calf head from which it is made is often called a turtle head. It is a complicated soup to make but was once a highly valued Victorian delicacy.

The halved calf's head is simmered until tender in water with a knuckle of bacon, chicken giblets, peppercorns, mace, pot vegetables and cloves. The meat is picked from the bones and the gelatinous stock is then strained and flavoured with sherry and pounded anchovies. Small pieces of the cooked veal are added to the soup before serving with delicate cheese straws.

Oxtail Soup

This soup was introduced by frugal Huguenot immigrants, who settled around Smithfield in the Sixteenth Century. They collected oxtails thrown out by meat merchants to make a nourishing meal, of which this is a modern version.

50 g/2 oz dripping
450 g/1 lb oxtail, cut into pieces
1 large onion, chopped
1 medium leek, chopped
1 large carrot, diced
1 large turnip, diced
2 tablespoons flour
1 bouquet garni
1 tablespoon tomato purée
1.4 litres/2½ pints water
1 tablespoon cornflour
150 ml/¼ pint brown ale

Melt the dripping in a large saucepan. Add the oxtail and vegetables and brown over a moderate heat. Stir in the flour, then add the bouquet garni, tomato purée and water. Bring to the boil, stirring constantly. Cover and simmer for 2½–3 hours, until the oxtail is really tender. Blend the cornflour with the brown ale, stir into the soup and bring back to the boil, stirring all the time. *Makes 6–8 servings.*

Fish

Whelks, cockles and jellied eels have always been enjoyed by Londoners, and still are today. Although the Thames is less productive of fish than it once was, a fish dinner at a riverside pub is still a possibility. You can board a river boat at Westminster Bridge for Greenwich to enjoy one of the famous whitebait dinners at the Trafalgar Tavern, recalling the good old days when the host would entertain Members of the Cabinet to a whitebait feast before the summer parliamentary recess, and mine host of the Old Ship Inn did the same for members of the Opposition.

Fried Whitebait

Wash and thoroughly dry the fish (which are in fact the small fry of herring or very small sprats). Toss them in seasoned flour in a bag until well coated, a few at a time, then deep fry at once in very hot fat until crisp and golden brown. Drain each batch and keep hot. When all are cooked, return them together to the frying basket and plunge again into the very hot fat for 1 minute to re-crisp. Drain well, sprinkle with salt, garnish with a sprig of parsley and serve immediately with lemon wedges. *Illustrated on the title page.*

Potted Sprats

1 kg/2 lb sprats
300 ml/½ pint white vinegar
150 ml/¼ pint water
1 teaspoon salt
¼ teaspoon pepper
¼ teaspoon ground mace
2 bay leaves
10 peppercorns
100 g/4 oz butter, melted

Remove the heads from the sprats and gut the fish. Wash in salted water and pat dry. Place in an ovenproof dish and pour over the vinegar and water. Season with the salt, pepper and mace and add the bay leaves and peppercorns. Bake in a moderate oven (180°C, 350°F, Gas Mark 4) for 45 minutes. Allow to cool, lift out the sprats and drain thoroughly. Pack tightly into small dishes and pour melted butter over the top. *Makes 6 servings.* *Illustrated overleaf.*

Arnold Bennett Omelette

This fish omelette was created by the Savoy Hotel to regale the famous theatre critic after the curtain had fallen. It is regarded as being an Epicurean dish, and like many such fancy dishes is very rich.

Butter and cream are liberally mixed with flaked smoked haddock and egg yolks, then with grated cheese and more cream. The stiffly whisked egg whites are folded in before cooking the omelette in the usual way. The unfolded omelette is topped with yet more cream and cheese and browned under the grill.

Stewed Eels and Mash with Parsley Sauce

The same parsley sauce was often served with meat pies and mash in Cockney eel-and-pie shops. The sauce went just as well with meat and was considered particularly tasty.

1 kg/2 lb eels
juice of 1 lemon
salt
Sauce
75 g/3 oz butter
75 g/3 oz flour
1 large bunch of parsley, finely chopped
salt and pepper

Remove the heads from the eels and soak the fish in salted water to cover for 15 minutes. Drain, remove the skins, wash the skinned eels again and cut them into 5-cm/2-inch pieces. Place in a saucepan, cover with water and add the lemon juice and salt to taste. Bring to the boil and simmer for 30 minutes.

Melt the butter in a clean pan and stir in the flour. Cook for 3 minutes. Gradually add sufficient liquid from cooking the eels to make a fairly thin white sauce. Stir in the parsley and cook gently for 5–10 minutes. Season to taste. Drain the pieces of eel, place in individual dishes and spoon over the sauce. Serve with plenty of mashed potato. *Makes 6 servings.*

Fish Pie

Fish caught all round the British Isles comes to London to be sold, so there is often a wide choice for the London housewife. A mixture of smoked and fresh fish is especially good in this pie.

450 g/1 lb smoked haddock
450 g/1 lb cod
40 g/1½ oz butter
40 g/1½ oz flour
300 ml/½ pint milk
1 teaspoon anchovy essence
75 g/3 oz cheese, grated
2 tablespoons chopped parsley
salt and pepper
675 g/1½ lb mashed potato

Place the fish in a large saucepan and just cover with cold water. Bring gently to the boil and simmer for 15–20 minutes. Drain and reserve 300 ml/½ pint of the cooking liquor. Flake the fish, discarding the bones, and place in an ovenproof dish.

Melt the butter and stir in the flour. Cook for 1 minute then stir in the milk and reserved fish liquor. Bring to the boil, stirring all the time, until the sauce is smooth and thickened. Cook for 1–2 minutes, stirring. Add the anchovy essence, cheese and parsley. Season to taste and pour over the fish. Season the potato and spread over the fish mixture. Mark the top with a fork and cook in a moderate oven (180°C, 350°F, Gas Mark 4) for 30–40 minutes, until golden brown on top. *Makes 6 servings.*

Jellied Eels

Fish stalls and eel-and-pie shops were a popular sight in the streets of London during the Nineteenth Century and the early part of this century. Innumerable stalls and shops, selling such local specialities as whelks and jellied eels, can still be found in the East End, Islington and Bermondsey.

1 kg/2 lb freshwater eel
1 litre/1$\frac{3}{4}$ pints water
5 tablespoons vinegar
2 teaspoons salt
1 bay leaf
1 small bunch of parsley stalks
1 teaspoon crushed peppercorns
1 onion, sliced
1 carrot, sliced

Skin and clean the eel. Cut into 1.5-cm/$\frac{3}{4}$-inch slices. Rinse thoroughly under cold running water and drain. Put the remaining ingredients in a saucepan and simmer uncovered for 30 minutes. Strain into a clean pan, add the eel slices, bring to boiling point and simmer for 15 minutes. Skim the surface if necessary. Allow the eel to cool in the liquid and jellify. Serve with boiled potatoes and horseradish sauce. *Makes* 4 *servings. Illustrated below right.*

Although the Thames is less productive of fish than it once was, a London fishmonger's slab has always displayed a good selection of city favourites. Two popular dishes were Jellied Eels (centre) and Potted Sprats (right).

HE OYSTER SEASON
HAS COMMENCED

Main Dishes

These run the gamut from favourites which appealed to Dr. Johnson's gargantuan appetite through the family feasts of Dickens' novels to those which were celebrated in famous music hall ditties of the Edwardian era.

Veal Goose

In a large town like London, geese had to be brought in from the country. Flocks of them were even made to walk to London from as far away as Norfolk. Even in Hanoverian times they were therefore expensive and often rather scrawny, not surprising after such a long journey on foot. Veal and beef from Smithfield, on the other hand, were cheap meats and with this stuffing tasted somewhat like goose. They were often served with the traditional apple or bread sauce to heighten the illusion.

1 (1.75-kg/4-lb) boned shoulder of veal
1 medium onion
100 g/4 oz butter
175 g/6 oz dry white breadcrumbs
1 tablespoon chopped sage
salt and pepper

Flatten the veal slightly by beating with a rolling pin. Finely chop the onion. Melt half the butter in a saucepan and use to sweat the onion very gently until soft. Stir in the breadcrumbs, sage and seasoning to taste. Spread over the meat, roll it up and tie with string or secure with skewers. Place in a roasting tin, dot with the remaining butter and roast in a moderate oven (180°C, 350°F, Gas Mark 4) for 3 hours, or until the meat is tender, basting frequently. If necessary, more butter should be used to prevent the meat drying out. *Makes 8 servings.*

Mixed Grill

Chop Houses were some of the first London establishments to feature a mixed grill on their menus, pampering to the tastes of those who liked a little of all the different foods ready to be placed on the charcoal grill.

4 lamb chops, 2.5 cm/1 inch thick
4 lambs' kidneys, halved
4 slices lamb's or calf's liver
4 sausages
melted lard to brush
4 tomatoes, halved
12 flat mushrooms
salt and pepper
Garnish
sprigs of watercress
fried potatoes or crisps

The grill should be preheated. Trim the chops and nick the fatty edges to prevent them curling up. Place on the rack of the grill pan and grill for 5 minutes. Core the kidneys, add to the rack with the liver and sausages, brush with a little melted fat and grill for a further 5 minutes. Turn the food over, add the tomatoes and mushrooms, brush with fat and grill for a further 5 minutes. Season and serve with watercress and fried potatoes. *Makes 4 servings.*

Regent Lamb Chops

This dish was created for the Prince Regent, but with his enormous appetite a couple of loin chops could only have been enough for an appetiser. He probably ate the lot.

8 small lamb loin chops
8 rashers streaky bacon
8 shallots or button onions
salt and pepper
½ teaspoon ground rosemary
25 g/1 oz butter, melted
Sauce
225 g/8 oz redcurrants
50 g/2 oz castor sugar
6 tablespoons water

Remove the bone from each chop, leaving the meat in one piece to make a noisette. Shape into a circle, wrap a thin rasher of bacon around it and insert a shallot into the centre. Secure with skewers. Sprinkle each chop with salt, pepper and rosemary and brush with melted butter. Grill for 7–8 minutes on each side.

Meanwhile, boil the redcurrants and the sugar in the water for about 10 minutes, until the redcurrants are soft. Pour over the chops. *Makes 4 servings.*

Reform Club Sauce

This sauce was created by Alexis Soyer, the famous Nineteenth Century chef at the Reform Club. The colours of the various sauce ingredients—hard-boiled egg white, gherkin, beetroot and ham—were intended to echo the colours of the club's insignia.

1 onion
2 tablespoons vinegar
25 g/1 oz soft brown sugar
1 tablespoon crushed black peppercorns
300 ml/½ pint brown gravy or stock
1 tablespoon redcurrant jelly
2 thin slices ham or tongue
1 small beetroot, cooked
2 gherkins
1 hard-boiled egg white
salt and pepper

Finely chop the onion and place in a saucepan with the vinegar, sugar and peppercorns. Cook quickly until the onion is soft. Stir in the gravy or stock and the redcurrant jelly. Simmer for a few minutes, then strain into a clean pan. Cut the ham, beetroot, gherkins and egg white into matchstick strips. Add to the sauce, adjust the seasoning if necessary and heat through. Serve with grilled lamb cutlets or chops. *Makes about 300 ml/½ pint.*

Dowlet Pie

This old recipe for a meat pie was originally prepared without any seasoning, as not much distinction was made between the savoury or sweet dishes which followed the large joints. Dr. Johnson particularly enjoyed it, but he was not noted for his refined taste in food. During a meal, when this pie was also served, he is said to have poured lobster sauce over a rich fruit pudding, and enjoyed that as well!

1 kg/2 lb pie veal
salt and pepper
100 g/4 oz shredded suet
½ teaspoon ground mixed spice
1 teaspoon dried herbs
1 teaspoon sugar
1 egg, beaten
100 g/4 oz stoned dates
450 g/1 lb stoned plums
or 175 g/6 oz stoned prunes
150 ml/¼ pint sweet white wine
25 g/1 oz butter

Place the veal in a saucepan with enough water just to cover. Add a pinch of salt, bring to boiling point, cover and simmer for about 20 minutes, until the veal is almost tender. Drain, mince the meat and mix with the suet, spice, herbs and sugar. Add seasoning to taste, if liked. Bind with the egg to make a stiff paste. Form the mixture into balls, placing a date in the centre of each. Place in a pie dish with the plums.

Bring the wine and butter to the boil in a saucepan and pour over the pie. Bake in a moderate oven (180°C, 350°F, Gas Mark 4) for 30 minutes, until the plums are tender. *Makes 6 servings.*

Chicken Chop Suey

Chop Suey has been popular for almost a century in many great ports of the Western world, particularly where there is a resident Chinese population as in London. The name of this accommodating recipe really means quick to cook.

It may include chicken (or other meats), seafood, onion, bamboo shoots, beansprouts, water chestnuts and stock. The Port of London version usually includes fresh or canned tomato as well. The crisp vegetables are finely chopped or shredded and tossed in a little oil over low heat until just tender. These are pushed to the sides of the pan, then strips of chicken are added, chopped tomato flesh, stock and seasoning. When the chicken is tender, the chop suey is thickened with a little cornflour paste and sharpened with soy sauce and ginger. In a more expensive version, a little sherry is added and the dish is served topped with a thin omelette.

Madras Beef Curry

Indian restaurants have been a feature of the London scene since the early days of the East India Company. Indian food is traditionally less expensive than anything served in our own Chop Houses, and very filling. The connoisseur would bravely order a Madras Beef Curry, knowing it to be hot and strong.

A hot beef curry is made by frying cubes of tender beef in ghee (clarified butter) with chopped onion and garlic, stirring in curry powder to taste, lemon juice, stock, chutney and tomato pulp, and simmering until the meat is cooked. Sometimes the curry is thickened with a little flour and seasoned with salt. It is always served with plenty of freshly boiled long-grain rice and side dishes of sweet mango chutney, hot lime pickle and sliced raw onion.

Steak and Kidney Pudding

Steak and Kidney Pudding is made much as it was in Dickens' day, apart, that is, from the oysters and larks! The Cheshire Cheese off Fleet Street still serves a pudding reputed to be made from a recipe enjoyed by Dr. Samuel Johnson.

450 g/1 lb plain flour
pinch of salt
225 g/8 oz shredded suet
Filling
1 kg/2 lb stewing steak
225 g/8 oz lamb's kidney
6 tablespoons seasoned flour
100 g/4 oz button mushrooms
1 medium onion, chopped
4 tablespoons chopped parsley
about 150 ml/$\frac{1}{4}$ pint boiling water

First make the pastry. Sift the flour and salt into a bowl. Stir in the suet and add sufficient cold water (about 175–200 ml/6–7 fl oz) to make a firm dough.

Cut the steak and kidney into 2.5-cm/1-inch cubes. Place in a bowl and toss with the seasoned flour. Mix in the mushrooms, onion and parsley.

Roll out two-thirds of the pastry and use to line a 1.75-litre/3-pint pudding basin, or four 300-ml/$\frac{1}{2}$-pint pudding basins. Fill with the meat mixture, mounding it up slightly in the centre. Pour in the boiling water. Roll out the remaining pastry to make a lid, moisten the edges and pinch well to seal. Cover with a circle of greased greaseproof paper or foil with a pleat in the top and tie on securely. Steam for $3\frac{1}{2}$–4 hours. Wrap in a clean linen napkin, and serve from the basin. *Makes 8 servings. Illustrated left.*

Marrow Bones on Toast

Victorian Londoners enjoyed beef marrow on toast for tea as much as they did a good kipper or bloater. Veal or beef marrow bones were sawn up into sections by the butcher, then gently cooked standing upright in a saucepan of stock with flour and water paste over the cut ends. When the marrow was cooked, after about 30 minutes, the bones were lifted out and the paste removed. The cooked marrow was carefully pushed out with a long spoon and spread on hot buttered toast. Sometimes pieces of marrow were dipped into a rich batter and then fried.

Left
There's nothing like an old-fashioned pub lunch. Steak and Kidney Pudding has been enjoyed by Londoners since the days of Dr. Johnson, while Boiled Beef and Carrots has been a Cockney favourite for almost as long.

Boiled Beef and Carrots

It is said that Boiled Beef, a cherished Cockney dish, must be served with carrots, pease pudding and dumplings. The old music hall chorus extolling its virtues is still sung today.

1 (1.5-kg/$3\frac{1}{4}$-lb) joint boned brisket of beef
18 button onions
18 small whole carrots
1 bay leaf
salt and pepper
Dumplings
100 g/4 oz plain flour
$\frac{1}{2}$ teaspoon baking powder
generous pinch of salt
50 g/2 oz shredded suet
4 tablespoons milk

Put the brisket into a large saucepan and add sufficient cold water to completely cover it. Bring to the boil, skimming off any scum as it rises. Cover the pan and simmer for $2\frac{1}{2}$ hours. Add the onions, carrots, bay leaf and seasoning, bring back to the boil and simmer for a further 30 minutes.

To make the dumplings, sift the flour, baking powder and salt into a bowl. Stir in the suet and mix to a dough with the milk. Shape into walnut-sized balls. Remove the meat and vegetables to a serving dish and keep hot. Drop the dumplings into the hot cooking liquid and boil gently for 15–20 minutes. Serve with the meat and vegetables. *Makes 6 servings. Illustrated left.*

Mince Pies

Many myths and legends surround the mince pie. It was considered essential by some that twelve pies should be eaten between Christmas day and 'twelfth day', in order to ensure a lucky year. Although we now use only mixed dried fruits and suet, the original recipe included freshly minced meat. The fruits and spices helped to preserve the meat. Mince pies were originally oval in shape, not round, to represent the manger in which Jesus was laid, and contained three spices as a reminder of the gifts of the Three Kings.

Buns

In the South, a bun is something made from a yeasted bread mixture. Most famous of all is the Hot Cross Bun sold on Good Friday. It was popularly believed that the buns baked on that day should be hung up or dried out in a warm cupboard and saved until the next Easter festival. Stomach disorders and dysentery were prevalent in overcrowded London and a sovereign remedy was said to be a little of the hard bun grated and mixed with brandy and milk. This rhyme expresses the old superstition:

When Good Friday come, and old Woman runs
With one or two-a-penny Hot Cross Buns,
Whose Virtue is, if you believe what's said,
They'll not grow mouldy like the common Bread.

Hot Cross Buns

Many of our festive cakes have religious or mythological origins. The familiar cross on the Hot Cross Bun dates back to pre-Christian times. It is thought that the circular bun shape was intended to represent the sun, and that the cross divided it into quarters, representing the four seasons.

575 g/1¼ lb plain flour
1 teaspoon salt
½ teaspoon ground cinnamon
½ teaspoon freshly grated nutmeg
½ teaspoon ground mixed spice
50 g/2 oz butter
50 g/2 oz castor sugar
50 g/2 oz chopped mixed peel
100 g/4 oz currants
25 g/1 oz fresh yeast
275 ml/9 fl oz tepid milk
1 egg, beaten
Glaze
50 g/2 oz castor sugar
4 tablespoons water

Sift the flour, salt and spices into a bowl. Rub in the butter until the mixture resembles fine breadcrumbs. Stir in the sugar, peel and currants. Cream the yeast with a little of the milk, add the rest of the milk and the beaten egg. Make a well in the dry ingredients, add the yeast liquid and mix to a soft dough. Knead on a floured surface for 10 minutes, until smooth. Return to the bowl, cover and leave in a warm place for 1 hour, until double in size. Turn out on a floured surface and knead lightly. Divide into 12–14 pieces and shape each into a round bun. Arrange the buns on greased baking trays and cut a cross on the top of each, with a sharp knife. Leave in a warm place to prove for 15 minutes. Bake in a moderately hot oven (200°C, 400°F, Gas Mark 6) for 15–20 minutes, until well risen and golden brown.

Boil the sugar with the water, and as soon as the buns come out of the oven, brush them with the sugar glaze. These buns are delicious reheated in the oven and served warm with butter. *Makes 12–14. Illustrated overleaf.*

Chelsea Buns

'Captain Bun' was reputed to have sold thousands of buns every day, at his Old Chelsea Bun House in the Pimlico Road. George III and Queen Charlotte were two of his regular customers, and would stop their carriage outside to send in for some buns.

575 g/1¼ lb plain flour, warmed
pinch of salt
150 g/5 oz castor sugar
150 g/5 oz butter
25 g/1 oz fresh yeast
150 ml/¼ pint tepid milk
3 eggs, beaten
100 g/4 oz currants
1 teaspoon ground mixed spice
Glaze
50 g/2 oz sugar
2 tablespoons water

Sift the flour with the salt into a warm bowl. Stir in half the sugar. Rub in half the butter and make a well in the centre. Cream the yeast with 1 teaspoon sugar and gradually blend in the tepid milk and beaten eggs. Pour into the flour mixture and form into a dough. Turn out on a floured surface and knead until smooth. Return to the bowl, cover and leave in a warm place until double in size. Soften the remaining butter. Turn the dough out on a floured surface, knead lightly and roll into a rectangle about 1 cm/½ inch thick. Spread with the softened butter and sprinkle with half the remaining sugar. Fold the dough in half and roll out again to the same thickness. Sprinkle with the remaining sugar, the currants and the spice, and roll up from the long side, like a Swiss roll. Cut into 3.5-cm/1½-inch slices. Place close together, cut sides uppermost, on a warm, greased baking tray. Cover and prove in a warm place for 20 minutes. The buns should now be touching. Bake in a moderately hot oven (200°C, 400°F, Gas Mark 6) for 30 minutes.

To make the glaze, boil the sugar with the water. Glaze the buns with the syrup as soon as they come out of the oven. Leave to cool before separating. *Makes about 12. Illustrated overleaf.*

London Buns

London Buns (also called Johnny Cakes) are what we now refer to as Swiss Buns – large fingers, coated with a thick white icing. The original recipe omitted the icing and the buns had a distinctive spicy flavour.

1 kg/2 lb plain flour
pinch of freshly grated nutmeg
100 g/4 oz castor sugar
75 g/3 oz butter
600 ml/1 pint milk
25 g/1 oz fresh yeast
50 g/2 oz chopped mixed peel
Glaze
1 egg, beaten
2 tablespoons granulated sugar

Sift the flour and nutmeg into a warm bowl, stir in the castor sugar and make a well in the centre. Heat the butter with the milk until the butter melts. Allow to cool until just warm. Cream the yeast and gradually blend in the tepid milk. Pour into the flour mixture with the peel and mix to a dough. Cover and leave in a warm place until double in size. Turn out on a floured surface, knead well and form into 24 finger-shaped buns. Arrange on greased baking trays, cover and leave in a warm place until double in size. Bake in a moderately hot oven (200°C, 400°F, Gas Mark 6) for about 25 minutes. To make the glaze, mix the egg with the sugar and use to brush the tops of the buns. Return to the oven for a further 5 minutes, to set the glaze. *Makes 24. Illustrated overleaf.*

Muffins

The muffin and crumpet sellers of London are amongst the oldest of street traders, and the ringing of their bells was a familiar sound right up to the 1930's. Children used to sing a favourite rhyme which ended (along with much energetic miming of ringing a hand bell) with the words 'Do you know the muffin man who comes down Drury Lane?'

450 g/1 lb plain flour
1 teaspoon salt
25 g/1 oz fresh yeast
275 ml/9 fl oz tepid milk
1 egg, beaten
25 g/1 oz butter, melted

Sift the flour and salt into a bowl. Cream the yeast with a little of the milk, add the rest of the milk and the beaten egg. Make a well in the dry ingredients, add the yeast liquid and melted butter and mix to a soft dough. Turn out on a floured board and knead for 10 minutes, until smooth. Cover and leave in a warm place until double in size. Turn out on a floured board and knead lightly. Roll out to 1 cm/½ inch thickness and cut into rounds with a 7.5-cm/3-inch cutter. Place on a floured board and dust the tops with flour. Cover and leave in a warm place until double in size. Cook the muffins, a few at a time, on a greased girdle or in a thick frying pan, over moderate heat, for about 8 minutes on each side. Serve warm, split and spread with butter. *Makes about 10. Illustrated overleaf.*

Kensington Roll

The Royal Borough of Kensington has long been considered a genteel and wealthy area, where patrons of the better class bakeries were prepared to pay well for teatime delicacies. This enriched bun is far more expensive than the simple London Bun and is reputed to have graced the tea-table of the young Princess Victoria at Kensington Palace in the early 1830's.

15 g/½ oz fresh yeast
150 ml/¼ pint warm milk
450 g/1 lb plain flour
1 teaspoon salt
50 g/2 oz castor sugar
100 g/4 oz butter
3 eggs, beaten
225 g/8 oz almond paste
To Decorate
glacé icing
chopped almonds or
'hundreds and thousands'

Blend the yeast with the milk and allow to stand in a warm place for about 15 minutes, until frothy. Sift the flour and salt into a bowl. Stir in the sugar. Rub in the butter, add the yeast liquid and beaten eggs and mix to a soft dough. Turn out on a floured surface and knead until the dough is elastic and no longer sticky. Form into a ball, cover and leave in a warm place until double in size. Turn out on a floured surface and knead lightly. Roll out the dough to a rectangle about 25 × 35 cm/10 × 14 inches, and roll out the almond paste to the same size. Place on the dough and roll up like a Swiss roll, from the long side. Place on a greased baking tray, cover and leave in a warm place until double in size. Bake in a hot oven (220°C, 425°F, Gas Mark 7) for 15 minutes. Allow to cool. Decorate with glacé icing and chopped almonds or 'hundreds and thousands'. Serve cut in slices like a Swiss roll. *Makes 16–18 slices. Illustrated overleaf.*

RASSO
ETAL
OLISH
WOODBINE

Above
Nell Gwyn's Orange Jellies
Left
Not only the Chelsea Pensioners would be proud of this impressive spread of London's buns. From left: Chelsea Buns, London Buns, Kensington Roll, Muffins and Hot Cross Buns.

Nell Gwyn's Orange Jellies

Oranges sold to the audience at the Theatre Royal in the days of Charles II were used to pelt unpopular actors on the stage. These golden fruits were also enjoyed by Samuel Pepys and his friends in this sweet confection.

4 medium oranges
2 tablespoons sherry
1 lemon
25 g/1 oz gelatine
100 g/4 oz sugar

Pare the rind thinly from one of the oranges and soak in the sherry for 1–2 hours. Cut each orange in half and, using a teaspoon and holding the orange firmly in one hand, remove the flesh, taking care not to pierce the skin. Reserve the unpared shells to use as containers. Squeeze the pared orange shell and the lemon. Remove the rind from the sherry and discard it. Dissolve the gelatine in a basin in 4 tablespoons of water over a pan of hot water. Combine the fruit juices, sherry and sugar in a saucepan and heat gently until the sugar has dissolved. Stir in the gelatine and fruit pulp and spoon into the orange shells. Chill until firmly set. Cut each jelly in half to make 12 small boat shapes filled with jelly. *Makes 3–4 servings. Illustrated above.*

Note A similar jelly, made in larger quantities and set in a mould, was a traditional Christmas dish in Yorkshire, where it was served with whipped cream and lemon cheesecakes.

Sweets

Londoners have always preferred rich and refined sweets to the more filling puddings of the North.

Westminster Fool

Take 8 thin slices from a small currant loaf and place in the bottom of a serving dish. Moisten with sweet sherry. Beat 3 eggs well, stir in a little ground mace and a teaspoon of rose water. Sweeten with castor sugar to taste and stir in 600 ml/1 pint of fresh milk or single cream. Pour into a double saucepan and stir over simmering water until it forms a custard which will coat the back of the spoon. Cool, and when the custard thickens, pour into the serving dish. Allow to cool and set. *Makes 4 servings.*

Boodle's Orange Fool

London clubs have claimed many attributes over the years. A certain Mrs. Gore was known to say: 'London clubs, after all, are not bad things for family men. The man forced to remain at home, and vent his crossness on his wife and children, is a much worse animal to bear with than the man who grumbles his way to Pall Mall.'

Many clubs, such as Boodle's in St. James, have gained a reputation for serving good food.

4 large oranges
2 lemons
2–3 tablespoons castor sugar
6 trifle sponge cakes
600 ml/1 pint double cream

Finely grate the rind from 2 oranges and 1 lemon. Squeeze the juice from all the fruit and add sugar to taste. Cut each sponge cake into four and place in a serving bowl. Mix the cream with the fruit juices and grated rind. Pour over the sponge cake and chill for 2 hours. *Makes 6 servings.*

Raspberry Lockets

Another old recipe from one of the famous London Clubs, Lockets, this was very popular in summer and early autumn when the Scottish raspberries were sent south.

The fruit is arranged in glass dishes, sprinkled with Kirsch and completely covered with whipped cream. Then a layer of demerara sugar is sprinkled on top and a red hot skewer can be drawn across the surface in a diamond pattern to caramelise it. *Illustrated on the title page.*

Thatched House Tavern Rice Pudding

This rather solid pastry sweet was served at the Thatched House Tavern in St. James's. The recipe is said to date from the time of William of Orange.

50 g/2 oz short-grain rice
450 ml/¾ pint milk
50 g/2 oz butter
350 g/12 oz prepared puff pastry
4 eggs
100 g/4 oz castor sugar
pinch of ground cinnamon
3 tablespoons double cream
little freshly grated nutmeg

Simmer the rice in the milk until tender but not mushy, stirring occasionally to separate the grains. Remove from the heat, stir in the butter and cool. Meanwhile, roll out the pastry and use to line a 1.25-litre/2-pint pie dish. When the rice mixture is cold, beat in the eggs, sugar, cinnamon and cream. Pour into the lined pie dish. Sprinkle lightly with nutmeg and bake in a hot oven (220°C, 425°F, Gas Mark 7) for 15 minutes, then reduce to 190°C, 375°F, Gas Mark 5 for a further 30 minutes, until well-risen and golden brown. Serve with cream or a purée of fruit. *Makes 6 servings.*

Lockshen Pudding

This most famous of all Jewish puddings has always had a place in the hearts of East End Cockneys, who like their food to be solid and filling. Bloom's in Whitechapel make the authentic pudding and members of our own Royal Family have been known to join the queue to enjoy it.

225 g/8 oz broad noodles
75 g/3 oz butter, melted
2 eggs, beaten
75 g/3 oz castor sugar
100 g/4 oz sultanas

Cook the noodles in boiling salted water for about 10 minutes, until just tender. Drain the cooked pasta and mix with the butter, eggs, sugar and sultanas. Pour into a greased ovenproof dish and bake in a moderately hot oven (190°C, 375°F, Gas Mark 5) for 30 minutes. Serve hot with stewed fruit. *Makes 6 servings.*

Variation Grated apple, grated lemon rind, chopped nuts, spices and chopped glacé cherries are sometimes added to the pudding before baking.

Hokey-Pokey

The great Cockney food treats, sold outside the pub or in the local market on a Sunday morning, were saucers of whelks or jellied eels. Next to the whelk stall, in summer, could be found the hokey-pokey cart.

Nineteenth Century Italian immigrants did a roaring trade in custard ice cream. The carts were painted white, red and green (the Italian national colours) and were roofed with canvas awnings supported by twisted brass rods like metal barley sugar.

No one has satisfactorily solved the mystery of the name hokey-pokey, but the shape of the biscuit cornet in which it was served was that of the old paper 'poke' or cornet used in sweet shops.

75 g/3 oz sugar
600 ml/1 pint milk
2 egg yolks
few drops of vanilla essence
150 ml/¼ pint sweetened whipped cream
or 150 ml/¼ pint cornflour custard

Dissolve the sugar in the milk and bring almost to boiling point. Whisk the egg yolks and gradually whisk into the sweetened milk. Pour into the top of a double saucepan and stir over simmering water until the custard thickens. Do not allow it to boil. Cool. Place in a freezing tray and when half-frozen turn out and beat in the vanilla essence and the sweetened whipped cream. (The commercial ice cream was blended with a well-flavoured and coloured cornflour custard to make it go further.) Return to the freezing tray and freeze. *Makes 6 servings.*

Royal Cream

15 g/½ oz gelatine
4 tablespoons cold water
6 macaroons
8 egg yolks
225 g/8 oz castor sugar
1 litre/1¾ pints milk

Sprinkle the gelatine over the water and allow to soften. Crush the macaroons finely. Whisk the egg yolks and sugar together until light and creamy. Add the crushed macaroons. Bring the milk to the boil and whisk into the egg mixture. Pour into a double saucepan, and stir over simmering water until the custard will coat the back of a spoon. Remove from the heat and whisk in the gelatine until dissolved. Pour into a rinsed mould and chill until set. Alternatively, the cream can be set in individual 'pots'. *Makes 8 servings.*

Twelfth Night Cake

January 6th was at one time celebrated to the same extent as Christmas Day. Twelfth Night marked the end of feasting when the decorations were taken down and a special entertainment was held, usually a play or masque. Traditionally, a rich fruit cake decorated with crystallised fruit was baked containing a single bean. The guest who got the slice containing this was called 'King of the Bean' and was supposed to have good luck throughout the coming year. An actor at Drury Lane Theatre called Robert Baddeley (who had previously been a cook) left a legacy to the theatre for a cake to be bought and eaten with a wine negus to be drunk in his memory in the Green Room, and this is still done today.

225 g/8 oz butter
225 g/8 oz castor sugar
4 eggs
3 tablespoons brandy or rum
225 g/8 oz plain flour
¼ teaspoon ground cinnamon
¼ teaspoon freshly grated nutmeg
225 g/8 oz currants
225 g/8 oz seedless raisins
100 g/4 oz sultanas
75 g/3 oz blanched almonds, chopped
1 dried bean (optional)

Cream the butter and sugar until light and fluffy. Whisk the eggs with the brandy and beat gradually into the mixture. Sift the flour and spices and add a little at a time, with the fruit and nuts. Beat until well mixed. Line a 25-cm/10-inch cake tin with buttered paper. Put in the mixture and smooth the top, making a slight hollow in the centre and inserting the bean if required. Bake in a cool oven (150°C, 300°F, Gas Mark 2) for 3–3½ hours. The cake is cooked when a thin skewer inserted in the centre comes out clean.

The Garden Counties

'All England is a garden', or so a poet claimed; but the spread of placid fields and orchards from London to the Channel certainly once resembled a vast market garden. Today, even though the area is bisected by busy roads and dotted with ever-spreading towns, it still serves as London's allotment.

Kentish cherries and Hampshire strawberries are as much in demand as Guernsey tomatoes and Jersey potatoes. Sussex has been famous for its succulent fruit, including figs, medlars and quinces, since medieval times. A day's outing from any part of London gives city dwellers a chance to pick their own produce at the height of the season – strawberries, raspberries, rhubarb, Brussels sprouts, peas and beans.

The sea is usually friendly to fishermen off the South Eastern coast of England. Chichester lobster, Selsey cockles and shrimps, Brighton plaice and Dover sole are all renowned for their superb quality. Some say there's nothing to compare with a Southdown saddle of lamb, tasting as it does of close-cropped thyme.

This is a rich, perhaps the richest of the ancient realms which together made up Olde England. The garden counties lie snugly around London, Britain's heart and focal point of commerce. There has never been poverty or lack of food here compared with the harsher North. Because the climate is more temperate, and the landscape less hilly and wooded, the soil tends to be more intensively cultivated. Mixed farming exists side by side with market gardening, and meat is never scarce. Local traditions abound for serving a boar's head at a feast, or roasting an ox at the annual fair.

Although Aylesbury duck is supposed to be the finest, many farms in this area boast a duck pond. All the specialities of this region tend to have a rich, expensive touch. Perhaps this is due in part to the number of great historic houses and royal palaces which nestle in the Thames Valley area – from Sheen through Richmond to Hampton and Windsor. There are regional dishes in plenty for merrymaking; for beanfeasts, harvest suppers, midsummer fêtes and fairs.

A Kentish cherry orchard in blossom.

Canterbury Cream of Mushroom Soup

Field mushrooms, with their rich flavour, abound towards the end of summer in the fertile fields of Southern England, and these are the kind to use for this soup.

25 g/1 oz butter
225 g/8 oz mushrooms, sliced
1 medium onion, chopped
600 ml/1 pint chicken stock
25 g/1 oz flour
450 ml/¾ pint milk
salt and pepper
4 tablespoons single cream
1 tablespoon chopped parsley

Melt the butter in a saucepan. Add the mushrooms and onion and cook gently until soft. Add the stock. Blend the flour with a little of the milk and gradually add to the pan with the rest of the milk, stirring well. Season to taste. Bring just to the boil, stirring all the time, then cover and simmer for 45 minutes. Just before serving, adjust the seasoning if necessary, stir in the cream and serve sprinkled with parsley. *Makes 4 servings.*

Brown Windsor Soup

This much maligned soup was reputedly a great favourite with Queen Victoria and frequently topped the menu in the early dining cars of the railways. At its honest best it is delicious and it would be a pity to equate it with the tasteless and rather suspiciously bright brown concoction once served all too often in cheap boarding houses.

25 g/1 oz butter
225 g/8 oz shin of beef, diced
1 small onion, chopped
1 small carrot, sliced
25 g/1 oz flour
1.15 litres/2 pints beef stock
1 bouquet garni
3 tablespoons Madeira
salt and pepper

Heat the butter in a saucepan and use to brown the meat, onion and carrot. Sprinkle in the flour and cook for a further 3–5 minutes, until golden brown. Gradually stir in the stock, and bring to the boil, stirring constantly. Add the bouquet garni, cover and simmer for 2 hours.

Remove the bouquet garni, press the soup through a sieve or liquidise in a blender. It should be smooth and fairly thick. Reheat and add the Madeira. Adjust the seasoning if necessary and serve accompanied by triangles of toast or warm rolls. *Makes 6 servings. Illustrated overleaf.*

Carp with Onions and Mushrooms

Monasteries were often famous for their carp ponds, where the fish were bred for the table. Before cooking, the fish should be soaked in water to remove the muddy smell and flavour.

1 carp (about 1.5–1.75 kg/3–4 lb)
little vinegar
50 g/2 oz butter
4 medium onions, sliced
600 ml/1 pint fish stock
225 g/8 oz button mushrooms
1 faggot of herbs
salt and pepper
25 g/1 oz flour

Have the fish gutted, cleaned and scaled, then soak in water with a little added vinegar for 2 hours. Pat dry and cut into slices. Melt half the butter in a saucepan, add the onion and fry gently until soft. Stir in the stock, mushrooms, herbs and seasoning. Bring to the boil, add the carp and simmer for 30 minutes, or until the fish is tender. Lift the fish pieces carefully on to a warm serving dish and keep hot. Mix the remaining butter with the flour to make a smooth paste. Add this a little at a time to the boiling stock and vegetables, stirring continuously, until the sauce thickens. Remove herbs, pour sauce over the fish and serve. *Makes 6–8 servings.*

Eel-Pie Island Eel Pie

Eel-Pie Island in the Thames was a great gathering place for picnickers, anglers and boating parties, who bought pies made with locally caught eels at the inn.

2 eels
1 onion, finely chopped
75 g/3 oz butter
4 tablespoons chopped parsley
pinch of freshly grated nutmeg
salt and pepper
4 tablespoons dry sherry
3 eggs, hard-boiled and sliced
50 g/2 oz flour
juice of 1 lemon
225 g/8 oz prepared puff pastry
beaten egg to brush

Skin, clean and bone the eels. Cut into small pieces. Finely chop the onion and fry gently in 25 g/1 oz butter until soft. Stir in the parsley, nutmeg, seasoning and sherry. Add the eel with sufficient water to just cover. Bring slowly to boiling point. Remove the pieces of eel and place in a deep 1.25-litre/2-pint pie dish with the sliced egg. Blend the remaining butter and the flour to a paste. Heat the cooking liquid and whisk in the kneaded butter in small pieces. Bring to the boil, whisking all the time. Add the lemon juice and pour the sauce over the eel mixture. Roll out the pastry to form a lid. Roll out the trimmings and use to make a pastry strip for the rim of the dish. Dampen and press on well. Cover with the pastry lid, dampen all edges and pinch to seal. Make a vent and brush with beaten egg. Bake in a hot oven (220°C, 425°F, Gas Mark 7) for 15 minutes, then reduce to moderately hot (190°C, 375°F, Gas Mark 5) for a further 40–45 minutes, until a rich brown. Serve hot or cold. *Makes 6 servings.*

Twice Laid

225 g/8 oz cod fillet, cooked
450 g/1 lb mashed potato
salt and pepper
milk to mix
1 egg, beaten
dry breadcrumbs to coat
deep fat or oil to fry

Remove any skin and bones from the cod then flake and mix with the mashed potato. Season well and add just sufficient milk to bind. Divide the mixture and form into the shape and size of eggs. Dip these in the beaten egg, coat in breadcrumbs and fry in deep hot fat or oil until golden brown all over. *Makes 4 servings.*

A Fricassey of Eggs

This was a very rich supper dish, usually made on the farm where all the ingredients were to hand.

10 eggs
100 g/4 oz butter
300 ml/½ pint double cream
salt and pepper

Hard-boil the eggs, shell them and cut eight into quarters lengthways. Heat the butter and cream until really hot, thick and smooth. Lay the egg quarters in the bottom of a serving dish. Season the sauce and pour over the eggs. Take the whites from the remaining eggs, chop them and pile in the centre. Sieve the yolks and sprinkle round the edge of the dish. *Makes 4–6 servings.*

Mumbled Eggs

A Regency dish of scrambled eggs was made with a spoonful or two of cream to each egg, well seasoned with salt and pepper, and served with large fried field mushrooms. At the houses of the gentry this delicious breakfast dish was served with asparagus instead of mushrooms.

Windsor Bean Pudding

Broad beans used often to be known as Windsor beans, and they grow very well in that district.

675 g/1½ lb shelled broad beans
salt and freshly ground pepper
2 egg yolks
25 g/1 oz butter
50 g/2 oz fresh white breadcrumbs
2 tablespoons single cream

Cook the beans in boiling salted water for 20 minutes, until tender. Drain and pound to a paste or liquidise in a blender. Season with salt and pepper, beat in the egg yolks, butter, breadcrumbs and cream. Tie the mixture in a floured cloth and cook in boiling water for 30 minutes. Squeeze out any surplus water and serve very hot.

Alternatively, steam the pudding for 30 minutes in a basin covered with greased greaseproof paper or foil, or place in an ovenproof dish and bake in a moderate oven (180°C, 350°F, Gas Mark 4) for the same length of time. *Makes 6 servings.*

Kidneys in Onions

4 large onions
4 sheep's or lamb's kidneys
salt and pepper
900 ml/$1\frac{1}{2}$ pints beef stock
2 tablespoons rum (optional)
4 sprigs of parsley

Peel the onions carefully, cut a slice from the top of each. Using a sharp knife hollow out the centres so that a kidney will fit inside. Reserve the onion which has been removed. Skin the kidneys, remove the cores and put one into each of the prepared onions. Season well and put back on the onion tops. Stand in an ovenproof casserole, add the reserved onion and pour in sufficient stock to come just over halfway up the sides of the onions. Cover and cook in a moderate oven (160°C, 325°F, Gas Mark 3) for $1\frac{1}{2}$ hours. Spoon the rum over the onions 30 minutes before the end of the cooking time.

Serve the onions garnished with parsley, with plenty of the gravy and hot buttered toast. *Makes 4 servings. Illustrated right.*

Mushrooms in Cream

50 g/2 oz butter
450 g/1 lb button mushrooms, sliced
salt and pepper
25 g/1 oz flour
300 ml/$\frac{1}{2}$ pint single cream

Melt the butter in a saucepan, add the mushrooms, season with salt and pepper, cover and cook gently for 10 minutes. Stir in the flour and cook for 3 minutes. Heat the cream until almost boiling, add it gradually to the mushroom mixture, stirring all the time. Adjust the seasoning and serve very hot with fried bread, if liked. *Makes 4–6 servings. Illustrated right.*

Right
In earlier days, the elegant first class dining cars of the railways frequently featured Brown Windsor Soup on the menu. Also shown are Mushrooms in Cream, a delicious savoury, and Kidneys in Onions, a dish originally served to sailors in a Southampton inn.

2503
Gt. Western Ry.
Paddington 2
Gt. Western Ry.
Paddington 2
WINDSOR & ETON
TO
Via Slough
FIRST CLASS
4/6
Fare
4/6
Windsor&Eton
Windsor&Eton
2503

Mushroom Circles

75 g/3 oz butter
8 large flat mushrooms
8 thick slices white bread
little made mustard

Melt 25 g/1 oz butter in a frying pan over moderate heat. Add the mushrooms and fry gently on both sides. Remove from the pan and keep hot. Cut the bread slices into eight rounds. Butter the bread rounds on one side and spread lightly with mustard. Add the rest of the butter to the frying pan and, when hot, put in the rounds of bread, unbuttered side downwards. Fry until the base is crisp and golden. Place a mushroom on each and serve very hot. *Makes 4 servings.*
Note Smaller mushrooms used in the same way make ideal savouries to end a meal.

Pickled Mushrooms

This is an ideal recipe for the small button mushrooms available all round the year.

600 ml/1 pint malt vinegar
2 blades mace
(or ¼ teaspoon ground mace)
6 peppercorns
1 kg/2 lb small button mushrooms
1 teaspoon salt

Bring the vinegar slowly to the boil with the mace and peppercorns. Put the mushrooms into a heavy pan, sprinkle with the salt and place over a gentle heat until the juices run. Continue heating until this liquid has evaporated. Pour on the strained vinegar and pot at once in small jars, making sure that the mushrooms are below the level of the liquid. Cover when cold. These pickled mushrooms are ready for eating after about 3 weeks. *Makes 1 kg/2 lb.*

Stewed Watercress

This can be served as a sauce with boiled fowl, or with stock added it becomes a nourishing soup.

Wash a bunch of watercress well in salted water, shake dry and boil in sufficient water to cover for 15 minutes. Drain well and chop finely, including the stalks. Melt 25 g/1 oz butter in a saucepan, add the chopped cress, season to taste with salt and pepper and cook gently in its own juices until quite tender. Stir in 1 teaspoon vinegar and serve as a sauce, or add 600 ml/1 pint well-seasoned stock from boiling a fowl and serve as a soup. *Makes 4 servings.*

Kentish Chicken Pudding

This recipe was devised to make good use of an old fowl when its egg-laying days were over. If a fowl was not available, the pudding was made with pigeons or rabbit and for special occasions strips of ham and mushrooms were also added.

450 g/1 lb self-raising flour
1 teaspoon salt
225 g/8 oz shredded suet
Filling
450 g/1 lb salt belly of pork
1 boiling fowl
2 large onions, chopped
1 teaspoon chopped parsley
salt and pepper
300 ml/½ pint chicken stock

Sift the flour and salt into a bowl, stir in the suet and mix with sufficient water to make a fairly stiff dough. Roll out three-quarters of the pastry and use to line a greased 1.75-litre/3-pint pudding basin.

Place the pork in a saucepan, cover with water, bring to the boil then drain and dice. Divide the fowl into eight portions.

Put the chicken portions, pork, onion, parsley and seasoning into the lined basin. Pour over the chicken stock. Roll out the remaining pastry to make a lid. Moisten the edges and seal well together. Cover with greased greaseproof paper or foil with a pleat in the centre and tie under the rim. Stand the pudding in a pan and add boiling water to come halfway up the sides of the basin. Boil for 3 hours, adding more water when necessary. Turn out on to a hot serving dish and accompany with vegetables and parsley sauce. *Makes 8 servings.*

Ashdown Partridge Pudding

225 g/8 oz self-raising flour
pinch of salt
100 g/4 oz shredded suet
Filling
1 brace of partridge, cleaned
salt and pepper
100 g/4 oz mushrooms, chopped
pinch of dried mixed herbs
1 teaspoon chopped parsley
100 g/4 oz rump steak, thinly sliced
150 ml/¼ pint claret or dry red wine
150 ml/¼ pint beef stock

Sift the flour and salt into a bowl. Stir in the shredded suet and add sufficient cold water to make a fairly stiff dough. Roll out two-thirds of the pastry and use to line a greased 1-litre/1¾-pint pudding basin.

Cut the partridges into neat small portions and mix with some salt and pepper, the chopped mushrooms and herbs. Put the steak into the base of the lined basin, add the partridge mixture and pour in the wine and stock. Roll out the remaining pastry to make a lid, dampen the edges and seal well. Cover with greased greaseproof paper or foil with a pleat in the centre and tie under the rim. Place in a saucepan and add sufficient boiling water to come half-way up the sides of the basin. Cook for 3–3½ hours, adding more boiling water when necessary. Serve from the basin. *Makes 6 servings.*

Ifield Vicarage Hogs' Puddings

450 g/1 lb pork
150 ml/¼ pint water
675 g/1½ lb plain flour
½ teaspoon salt
1 teaspoon baking powder
450 g/1 lb lard
450 g/1 lb currants
generous pinch of ground allspice
sausage skins

Cut the pork into small pieces and place in a pan with the water. Bring to the boil, cover and simmer for 1 hour, until the pork is tender. Sift the flour, salt and baking powder into a bowl. Rub in the lard. Stir in the meat, currants and spice with sufficient of the cooking stock to make a stiff dough. Fill the sausage skins with this mixture and tie in bunches. Prick the puddings with a fork, drop into a pan of boiling water and simmer for 1½ hours. Remove from the pan and hang up to dry. The puddings are delicious eaten hot or cold as a savoury. *Makes about 8.*

Collared Beef

1 kg/2 lb salt beef
2 tablespoons chopped parsley
½ teaspoon dried sage
½ teaspoon dried mixed herbs
½ teaspoon ground allspice
¼ teaspoon cayenne pepper
salt and pepper

Remove any gristle from the meat. Mix together the parsley, sage, mixed herbs, allspice, cayenne and seasoning and use to coat the meat, pressing in well. Roll up tightly and bind with string or secure with skewers. Tie in a muslin cloth and place in a saucepan. Add cold water to cover and bring to the boil. Cover and simmer for about 4 hours, or until the meat is tender. Remove from the pan and place in a dish of suitable size, still in the muslin cloth. Put a heavy weight on top and leave until quite cold. Remove the weight and muslin cloth. Slice and serve with a salad. *Makes 6 servings.*

Note: This dish may also be served hot with horseradish or parsley sauce.

Southdown Shepherd's Pie

25 g/1 oz butter
1 large onion, chopped
1 teaspoon chopped thyme
1 tablespoon chopped parsley
450 g/1 lb cooked lamb, minced
300 ml/½ pint thick brown gravy
salt and freshly ground black pepper
675 g/1½ lb mashed potato

Melt half the butter and use to fry the onion until soft. Stir in the herbs, meat and gravy. Season to taste and place in an ovenproof dish. Season the potato and spread over the lamb mixture. Mark the surface with a fork to look like thatching. Dot with the remaining butter and cook in a moderate oven (180°C, 350°F, Gas Mark 4) for about 45 minutes, until the top is crisp and golden brown. *Makes 4–6 servings. Illustrated right.*

Mutton Pies

These are usually made with shortcrust pastry in a small size suitable for one person. They are frequently referred to in literature since the days of Chaucer, being the pies sold hot in the streets of Medieval towns by piemen, who returned to the baker's shop for fresh supplies as soon as their trays were empty.

Scotch Mutton Pies

These are a homelier version, well known under this name all over the country.

They are made with hot water crust pastry (see page 79), used to line large patty tins – the kind that come in fours and are usually mistaken for Yorkshire pudding tins – or raised round the housewife's clenched fist or small jam jars. Miniature ones are raised round the end of a thin rolling pin. The meat filling is finely chopped or minced mutton and sheep's kidney, seasoned with salt and pepper and moistened with a little stock. The mixture is packed firmly into the pastry cases, covered, glazed with milk and baked in a moderately hot oven (200°C, 400°F, Gas Mark 6) for about 1 hour. *Illustrated right.*

Right
Although shepherds are no longer to be seen wandering the Downs, at least one glorious legacy, Southdown Shepherd's Pie, survives unchanged. It is now as familiar all over the country as these Scotch Mutton Pies (foreground) which have been known since the days of Chaucer.

Strawberry Shortcake

175 g/6 oz self-raising flour
100 g/4 oz butter
100 g/4 oz castor sugar
1 egg, beaten
675 g/1½ lb strawberries
icing sugar to sweeten
300 ml/½ pint double cream

Sift the flour into a bowl and rub in the butter until the mixture resembles fine breadcrumbs. Stir in the sugar and mix to a dough with the egg. Knead lightly and divide into two equal portions. Shape each one into a flat round and place on a greased baking tray. Bake in a moderate oven (180°C, 350°F, Gas Mark 4) for 15 minutes, until firm to the touch. Cool on the baking tray.

Halve the strawberries and sweeten with sugar to taste. Place one of the cakes on a serving plate, cover with half the strawberries. Put the other cake on top and spread with the remaining berries. Whip the cream and use to cover the shortcake all over. *Makes 8 servings.*

Kentish Fruit and Cream

This county is famed for all sorts of soft fruit. Although often served simply with sugar and cream, fruit is also cooked according to this old farmhouse recipe.

225 g/8 oz preserving sugar
225 g/8 oz redcurrants
100 g/4 oz white currants
225 g/8 oz raspberries
225 g/8 oz strawberries
600 ml/1 pint double cream

Place the sugar in a saucepan. Strip the currants from the stalks and hull the berries. Add the currants to the sugar and place over gentle heat, stirring occasionally, until the juice runs. Bring to the boil and cook fairly quickly, stirring from time to time, until it becomes a thick syrup. Add the berries and cook for a further 2–3 minutes. Sieve and then cool the purée. Whip the cream until thick but not stiff and combine with the fruit purée. Turn into a large glass bowl or individual dessert glasses and chill before serving. *Makes 6–8 servings.*
Note If white currants are not available, increase the quantity of redcurrants.

Mulberries, Medlars and Quinces

These old-fashioned fruits may still be found in country gardens and orchards. The mulberry can be used in many recipes to replace raspberries or blackberries. Medlars have a papery skin and are not fit to eat until 'blelted', that is brown, soft and very ripe. They can be eaten with nuts or port and make a very good comfit (sweetmeat) or jelly. Quinces, though seldom grown now, are delicious simply stewed with sugar. When cold the juice sets to a lovely jelly. They are often combined with apples to make a compote.

Quince Custard Pie

450 g/1 lb quinces
about 150 ml/¼ pint water
100 g/4 oz castor sugar
¼ teaspoon ground cinnamon
2 teaspoons lemon juice
300 ml/½ pint double cream
3 egg yolks
225 g/8 oz prepared puff pastry

Peel and core the quinces. Cook them in the water until reduced to a pulp. Stir in the sugar, cinnamon and lemon juice. Cool. When cooled, stir in the cream and beaten egg yolks. Roll out the pastry and use to line a 20-cm/8-inch pie dish. Pour in the quince custard and bake in a hot oven (220°C, 425°F, Gas Mark 7) for 15 minutes, then reduce the heat to moderately hot (190°C, 375°F, Gas Mark 5) for a further 35 minutes. Serve cold. *Makes 4–6 servings.*
Note If quinces are not available, substitute 450 g/1 lb bananas, peeled and mashed to a pulp. Omit the water.

Osborne Pudding

This typically Victorian recipe is said to have been created for the royal nursery at Osborne, on the Isle of Wight. It is a delightful change from the stodgier bread and butter pudding made with dried fruit, and is also known locally as Jammy Pudding.

6 large slices slightly stale brown bread, trimmed
butter to spread
3 tablespoons raspberry or strawberry jam
50 g/2 oz soft brown sugar
2 eggs
600 ml/1 pint milk

Lightly butter the bread and spread the slices with jam. Lay the slices, jam side up, in a buttered pie dish, sprinkling a little sugar between the layers and on top. Whisk the eggs, then whisk in the milk until well blended. Pour over the bread and allow to stand for about 20 minutes, until the custard mixture is partially absorbed. Bake in a moderate oven (180°C, 350°F, Gas Mark 4) for 30–35 minutes, until the custard is just set. *Makes 4 servings.*

Vectis Pudding

225 g/8 oz self-raising flour
pinch of salt
100 g/4 oz shredded suet
Filling
2 medium cooking apples
50 g/2 oz sugar
50 g/2 oz currants
finely grated rind of 1 lemon
¼ teaspoon ground mixed spice
2 tablespoons golden syrup

Sift the flour and salt into a bowl, stir in the suet and sufficient cold water to make a stiff dough. Roll out on a floured surface to make a fairly thin large rectangle.

Peel, core and chop the apples and spread them over the pastry to within 2.5 cm/1 inch of the edges. Sprinkle with the sugar, currants, lemon rind and spice and trickle over the syrup. Moisten the edges, roll up like a Swiss roll and seal firmly. Wrap loosely in greased greaseproof paper or foil, seal the wrapping well and steam for 2 hours, adding more boiling water when necessary. Turn out on a hot dish and serve immediately. *Makes 4–6 servings.*

Apple Batter Pudding

175 g/6 oz plain flour
pinch of salt
4 eggs
300 ml/½ pint milk
6 small cooking apples
65 g/2½ oz butter
50 g/2 oz sugar
pinch of freshly grated nutmeg
½ teaspoon ground cinnamon
castor sugar to sprinkle

Sift the flour and salt into a bowl and make a well in the centre. Separate the eggs and stir the yolks into the flour. Gradually add the milk and a little water if necessary to make a thin creamy batter. Beat well and allow to stand for about 1 hour.

Peel and core the apples, taking care to leave them whole. Blend 50 g/2 oz of the butter with the sugar and spices and use to stuff the centres of the apples. Grease a pie dish with the remaining butter and place in the apples. Whisk the egg whites until stiff and fold gently into the batter. Pour over the apples and bake in a moderate oven (180°C, 350°F, Gas Mark 4) for about 1 hour, until the apples are tender and the batter is well risen. Serve hot sprinkled generously with sugar. *Makes 6 servings.*

Sussex Pond Pudding

The 'pond' is a delicious mixture of butter, sugar, lemon and fruit in the centre of the pudding. Leftover suet crust pastry can be made into 'swimmers': small dumplings cooked for about 20 minutes in boiling water, then slit and filled with a knob of butter and soft brown sugar for serving.

225 g/8 oz self-raising flour
100 g/4 oz shredded suet
150 ml/¼ pint water
Filling
100 g/4 oz soft brown sugar
100 g/4 oz mixed dried fruit
1 lemon
100 g/4 oz unsalted butter

Sift the flour into a bowl. Stir in the suet and add the water to make a soft dough. Roll out two-thirds of the dough to line a greased 1.5-litre/2½-pint pudding basin. Put half the sugar and fruit into the lined basin. Prick the lemon all over with a skewer and place upright on top. Cover with the butter in one piece and sprinkle over the remaining sugar and fruit. Roll out the rest of the pastry to make a lid. Moisten the edges and seal well together. Cover with greased greaseproof paper or foil with a pleat in the centre and tie under the rim of the basin. Place in a saucepan containing sufficient boiling water to come halfway up the sides of the basin. Cover and simmer for 2½ hours. Turn out on to a hot serving dish. Cut the pudding at the table to show the delicious buttery fruit syrup. Each serving should contain a portion of the lemon. *Makes 4–6 servings.*

Kentish Well Pudding In this variation the fruit is mixed into the pastry and the lemon is omitted from the butter filling.

The Cherry Orchard

In spring the orchards of Kent are dotted with the beautiful pink and white blossom of cherry trees. These cherries are the source of many delicious recipes, including some like Pickled Cherries which were invented to make use of fruit that was not suitable for dessert dishes or puddings.

Pickled Cherries

1.5 kg/3 lb red cherries, stoned
575 g/1¼ lb sugar
¼ teaspoon ground allspice
pinch each of ground cinnamon, nutmeg, mace and cloves
300 ml/½ pint white vinegar
150 ml/¼ pint water

Place the cherries in a saucepan with the sugar and spices. Pour over the vinegar and water and bring to the boil, stirring well. Simmer until the cherries are cooked but still firm. Strain and pack the cherries into clean, warmed jars. Boil the remaining syrup briskly until it thickens, then strain and pour over the fruit to cover. Cool before covering and sealing the jars. Serve with cold meats and poultry. *Makes about 1.75 kg/4 lb. Illustrated left.*

Cherry Stir-up Pudding

225 g/8 oz self-raising flour
pinch of salt
100 g/4 oz shredded suet
75 g/3 oz castor sugar
450 g/1 lb black cherries, stoned
milk to mix

Sift the flour and salt into a bowl. Stir in the suet, sugar and the cherries. Mix with enough milk to hold the mixture together. Shape into a roll on a floured surface and wrap in greased greaseproof paper or foil, allowing room for expansion. Seal the wrapping. Steam for 2–2½ hours.

Alternatively, press gently into a greased 20-cm/8-inch cake tin and bake in a moderate oven (180°C, 350°F, Gas Mark 4) for about 1½ hours, until well risen and firm to the touch. Serve with custard. *Makes 4–6 servings. Illustrated left.*

Left
The orchards of Kent are full of summer fruits, and when the cherry harvest is a good one, basketfuls will be gathered to turn into Cherry Stir-Up Pudding (left), Cherry Bumpers (right) and even Pickled Cherries (in the hamper).

Cherry Bumpers

These are served on Cherry Pie Sunday in early August to celebrate the end of the cherry picking season. They are served on baking trays still warm from the oven.

225 g/8 oz plain flour
pinch of salt
100 g/4 oz lard or margarine
Filling
450 g/1 lb ripe dark cherries, stoned
75 g/3 oz castor sugar

Sift the flour and salt into a bowl. Rub in the lard or margarine until the mixture resembles fine breadcrumbs. Add sufficient cold water to make a stiff dough. Roll out on a floured surface and cut into rounds about 10 cm/4 inches in diameter.

Place the cherries in a bowl and sprinkle with two-thirds of the sugar. Heap some of the cherries in the centre of each pastry round, draw the pastry up over the filling, dampen the edges and pinch firmly to seal. Place on a baking tray and bake in a moderately hot oven (200°C, 400°F, Gas Mark 6) for 20 minutes, until golden brown. Serve sprinkled with the remaining sugar. *Makes about 12. Illustrated on preceding pages.*

Cherry Pancakes

225 g/8 oz plain flour
pinch of salt
3 eggs
450 ml/¾ pint milk
butter or lard to fry
Filling
450 g/1 lb cherries, stoned
100 g/4 oz sugar
150 ml/¼ pint water
1 tablespoon cornflour
100 g/4 oz raspberries
1 tablespoon cherry brandy

Sift the flour and salt into a bowl, make a well in the centre, add the eggs and beat to a smooth paste with a little of the milk. Gradually add the remaining milk, beating constantly to make a smooth batter. Allow to stand for 30 minutes before using. Brush a shallow frying pan with fat and heat through evenly. Pour in just sufficient batter to cover the base of the pan. When golden brown underneath, loosen the pancake, toss or turn and brown the other side. Stack the cooked pancakes and keep warm.

To make the filling, put the cherries in a saucepan with the sugar and water. Bring to the boil and simmer until the cherries are tender. Moisten the cornflour with a little water, add to the pan and bring to the boil, stirring constantly. Simmer for 3 minutes. Stir in the raspberries and cherry brandy.

Fill the pancakes with the cherry mixture, roll up and place side by side in a shallow ovenproof serving dish. Spoon over any remaining cherry sauce. Place in a moderately hot oven (190°C, 375°F, Gas Mark 5) for about 15 minutes and serve warm with whipped cream. *Makes 6–8 servings.*

Note If the sauce is too thin, add an extra tablespoon of cornflour to thicken.

Poor Knights of Windsor

Most renowned of these 'poor knights' was Shakespeare's famous character, Sir John Falstaff. The original recipe included his favourite tipple, sack, a sweet wine from Spain, ancestor of our present-day sherry. The more common version uses ale instead or, for the truly indigent, milk with the sugar.

25 g/1 oz granulated sugar
150 ml/¼ pint warm ale
8 slices white bread, trimmed
3 egg yolks
3 tablespoons milk
75 g/3 oz butter
50 g/2 oz castor sugar
1 teaspoon ground cinnamon

Dissolve the granulated sugar in the ale and sprinkle over the bread slices. Beat the egg yolks with the milk and use to coat the bread slices. Melt the butter in a large pan and fry the slices until golden brown on both sides. Drain well and sprinkle with a mixture of castor sugar and cinnamon. Serve hot. *Makes 4 servings.*

Oast Cakes

225 g/8 oz plain flour
pinch of salt
1 teaspoon baking powder
50 g/2 oz lard
75 g/3 oz currants
1 teaspoon lemon juice
deep fat or oil to fry

Sift the flour, salt and baking powder into a bowl. Rub in the lard until the mixture resembles fine breadcrumbs. Add the currants and lemon juice and mix to a fairly stiff dough with a little water. Divide the dough into small pieces, form into balls and roll into circles on a floured board. Fry in hot fat or oil until golden brown all over. Drain well and serve hot. *Makes 4 servings.*

Richmond Maids of Honour

These pastry tarts were invented during the reign of Queen Elizabeth I by the cook at Hampton Court Palace and served to her Maids of Honour. The recipe remained a secret until Hanoverian times when a baker living in Richmond discovered what it was. He opened a shop near Kew Gardens where this delicious confection is still made and sold today.

450 g/1 lb prepared puff pastry
225 g/8 oz curd cheese
175 g/6 oz butter, softened
2 egg yolks
2 tablespoons brandy
175 g/6 oz castor sugar
1 large potato, baked in its jacket
50 g/2 oz ground almonds
1 lemon
little freshly grated nutmeg

Roll out the pastry on a floured surface and use to line about 24 bun tins. Break up the curd cheese with a fork and work in the softened butter. Beat together the egg yolks, brandy and sugar in another bowl. Remove the skin and mash the potato. Beat into the egg mixture with the ground almonds. Grate the rind from the lemon and squeeze the juice. Combine the cheese and egg mixtures, stir in the lemon rind and juice and the nutmeg. Mix well and spoon into the pastry cases. Bake in a moderately hot oven (190°C, 375°F, Gas Mark 5) for 30–40 minutes, until golden brown. *Makes about 24.*

Mothering Sunday Wafers

100 g/4 oz plain flour
75 g/3 oz castor sugar
4 tablespoons double cream
2 tablespoons orange flower water

Sift the flour into a bowl, add the sugar and stir in the cream and orange flower water. Beat thoroughly by hand for 10 minutes, or with an electric mixer for 6 minutes, until absolutely smooth. Spread spoonfuls of the mixture very thinly on greased baking trays. Bake in a moderately hot oven (200°C, 400°F, Gas Mark 6) for 6–8 minutes, until pale golden in colour. Leave for a few moments, then remove from the tray and curl each wafer round a rolling pin until firm. If they harden before curling, place the baking tray in the oven for a few moments to soften the wafers again.

Cool on a wire rack. When cold the wafers should be curved in shape and very crisp. Serve with jellies, fruit creams or ice creams. *Makes about 15.*

Fig and Rhubarb Jam

1 kg/2 lb dried figs
1.15 litres/2 pints water
1 kg/2 lb rhubarb, trimmed
grated rind and juice of 2 oranges
2.25 kg/5 lb preserving sugar

Cut the figs into small pieces and soak in the water for 24 hours. Cut the rhubarb into short lengths and place in a preserving pan with the figs and their soaking water. Bring to the boil and simmer until very soft. Remove from the heat and stir in the orange rind and juice and the preserving sugar. Stir until the sugar has dissolved. Return to the heat, bring back to the boil and boil rapidly, stirring occasionally to prevent sticking, and skimming if necessary. Test for setting by putting a little jam on a saucer and, when cool, pushing with the finger. When a set has been obtained, the surface will wrinkle. Cool the jam, stir to distribute the fruit and pot in clean, warmed jars. Cover and seal well. *Makes about 3.5 kg/8 lb.*

Rose Petal Jam

This rose petal jam never completely sets; it is really a thick conserve, delicious with milk puddings, as a topping for cereals, or spread on brown bread and butter.

450 g/1 lb preserving sugar
1 tablespoon water
450 g/1 lb fragrant red rose petals
2 teaspoons rose water

Heat the sugar with the water very slowly until dissolved, then bring to the boil to make a syrup. Wash and dry the rose petals and mix them with the rose water. Add to the syrup and simmer until the mixture thickens. Allow to cool, then pot in clean, warmed jars, cover and seal well. *Makes about 1 kg/2 lb.*

GLOSSARY

Ashet A dish on which meat is served.
Backstone, Bakestone A heavy stone or iron plate on which bread, scones, etc. are baked over an open fire.
Bag-in A meal taken to work by a farm worker.
Bannock A large, flat round of bread, scone or biscuit, the size of a dinner plate.
Bap A soft white bread roll, also known as a morning roll.
Bara brith Currant bread.
Barm Yeast.
Barm brack Sometimes called 'barm break', it is a speckled bread.
Bawd A hare.
Bree Broth or stock.
Bridie A pasty.
Broch, Brotch A spit.
Brose A dish of oatmeal mixed with boiling water.
Bubbly Jock A turkey.
Bumper A large turnover.
Buttermilk The liquid left after churning butter.
Buttery An enriched bread roll.
Chine The whole loin joint of bacon or pork.
Choppin A quart.
Clomed oben A clay-lined oven.
Collier's foot A pasty designed to fit into a miner's lunch box.
Collop A slice of boneless meat or a dish of minced meat.
Drover's bread A simple dough encasing strips of beef or sausages. Eaten by drovers on their long journeys.
Duff Dough.
Dutch oven A metal receptacle with a handle, and open on one side, used for baking scones, etc. in front of an open fire.
Fadge, Fage A large flat loaf or bannock.
Faggot (of herbs) A small bunch of herbs tied together, used for flavouring.
Farl One of the quarters or sections of a large bannock or scone.
Fatty cake A small enriched pastry cake.
Fired Cooked.
Flummery stick A wooden stick used for stirring oatmeal mixtures.
Fricassey A dish of poultry, rabbit, eggs, etc. in a sauce.
Gallimafray A hash or hotch potch.
Gigot, Jiggot A leg of mutton or lamb.
Girdle, Griddle A flat heavy iron baking plate, used over an open fire or on top of a stove.
Haggis A dish of liver, oatmeal, etc. cooked in a sheep's stomach bag.
Hob The top of the stove.
Hogmanay New Year's Eve.
Hotch potch A vegetable soup.
Hough Shin.
Huff paste A simple flour and water paste used to encase meat for cooking.
Jug To stew in a covered pot.
Junket A dish made from milk, sometimes flavoured, set with rennet.
Lancashire foot See Collier's foot.
Likky, Leeky A leek.
Neep Swede.
Oben, Hobbin, Ooben, Obbin An oven.
Oggy A Cornish name for pasty.
Partan A crab.
Planc A bakestone.
Plat A plate or dish.
Pluck Liver, heart, and lungs (lights) of food animals and birds. To pluck is also to remove feathers from birds.
Pot oven A simple large metal pot with a lid and short legs, used over an open fire.
Pot posy A faggot of herbs.
Pratie A potato.
Pudding pie An open flan or tart.
Purry A purée.
Sippet A small piece of toasted or fried bread used for garnishing.
Snap tin Tuck box.
Souse To pickle fish in a spiced solution of wine or vinegar.
Spurtle A smooth stick, sometimes decorated with a carved top, for stirring porridge.
Stay-bit A snack.
Syllabub A cold sweet of wine or cider whipped with cream or milk drawn straight from the cow.
Tappit hen A measure holding a quart.
Tattie A potato.
Tuck The food taken by a miner or other worker in his tuck-box or tin.
Turnover A semi-circular pasty.
Yule dough, dole or dows A small bread doll made at Christmas to represent the infant Jesus.

INDEX